JUNIOR HIGH SCHOOL
MATHS
STUDY DICTIONARY

Michael J Brown

PASCAL PRESS

Copyright © 2007 Michael J Brown
Reprinted 2008, 2009

ISBN 978 1 74125135 7

Pascal Press
PO Box 250
Glebe NSW 2037
(02) 8585 4044
www.pascalpress.com.au

Publisher: Vivienne Joannou
Project Editor: Linden Hyatt
Edited by Linden Hyatt
Indexed by Puddingburn Publishing Services
Answers checked by Peter Little
Typesetting and diagrams by Typecellars Pty Ltd
Illustrations by David Dickson
Cover by DiZign Pty Ltd
Printed by Green Giant Press

Reproduction and communication for educational purposes
The Australian *Copyright Act 1968* (the Act) allows a maximum of one chapter or 10% of the pages of this work, whichever is the greater, to be reproduced and/or communicated by any educational institution for its educational purposes provided that the educational institution (or the body that administers it) has given a remuneration notice to Copyright Agency Limited (CAL) under the Act.

For details of the CAL licence for educational institutions contact:

Copyright Agency Limited
Level 15, 233 Castlereagh Street
Sydney NSW 2000
Telephone: (02) 9394 7600
Facsimile: (02) 9394 7601
E-mail: enquiry@copyright.com.au

Reproduction and communication for other purposes
Except as permitted under the Act (for example a fair dealing for the purposes of study, research, criticism or review) no part of this book may be reproduced, stored in a retrieval system, communicated or transmitted in any form or by any means without prior written permission. All inquiries should be made to the publisher at the address above.

Every effort has been made to give the best or most accepted definitions of the entries in this study dictionary. If a reader has an alternative definition, please send it to the publisher together with the source or reference.

abacus

A

The letters A and a are used as pronumerals, labels and variables in maths.
The capital letter **A** stands for area in formulae.

For example, the area of a rhombus: $A = \frac{1}{2}ab$,
where a and b are the lengths of the two diagonals.

The capital letter A and other letters are
used in diagrams to name points,
lines and angles. See angle.

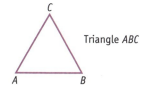

Triangle ABC

The lower case letter a and other letters are used as variables in algebra.

Q If $3a + 7 = 10$, find the value of a.
A $3a + 7 - 7 = 10 - 7$ (subtract 7 from each side)
$3a = 3$ and then $a = 1$
Note: $1a$ is written as a.

abacus
A calculating device consisting of beads on parallel wires within a frame. The most popular are the Chinese (shown) and Japanese.

abbreviation

algebraic: Allows the removal of × and ÷ symbols. See also simplify.

Q Write without × or ÷:
$5 \times a, x \times y, k \times k, x \div y$
A $5 \times a = 5a, x \times y = xy, k \times k = k^2, x \div y = \frac{x}{y}$

Excel Junior High School Maths Study Dictionary

 *abscissa*

index notation: A symbolic way to write repeated multiplications. Also called the **power** or **exponent**.

> **Q** Write in index notation: $a \times a \times a \times b \times b \times a \times b$ or $a.a.a.b.b.a.b$
> **A** $a.a.a.b.b.a.b = a^4 b^3$

in mathematics: There are special abbreviations. Here are the most common ones.
% percent **ie** that is **∴** therefore **∵** because
k thousands **eg** for example **am** *ante meridiem* **pm** *post meridiem*
  BC before Christ **AD** *anno domini*

abscissa The name of the horizontal or *x*-axis in the number plane. The value of the *x*-coordinate. The distance from the **y-axis**. See these entries also.

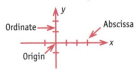

absolute addressing A computer **spreadsheet** term where a column and/or row can be locked so that an address in an equation will not change.

	A	B	C	D	E
1		Sophy	Todd	Bill	total
2	rent	15	20	15	50
3	gas	5	5	—	10
4	elec.	7	3	7	17
5	total	27	28	22	77

In this example C4 would always refer to Todd's electricity cost of $3.

absolute value The magnitude (size) of a value without regard to the sign.

> **Q** Find $|-3|$ and $|+3|$
> **A** $|-3| = |+3| = 3$

accuracy An indication of how far an approximate value may differ from a true value.
A measurement to the nearest $\frac{1}{100} = 0.01$ has a degree of accuracy of half of that measure, (±0.005).

> **Q** Give the accuracy of the measurement 3.1 cm.
> **A** The measurement is to one decimal place. Thus the accuracy is ±0.05 cm.

accurate A

accurate A value that is exact. Where there is no error. See **exact** also. √3 and π are exact while the usual representations of 1.73 and 3.14 respectively, are approximations of the actual values.

achilles and the tortoise One of the paradoxes of the Greek philosopher, Zeno. The paradox is important as it introduces the concept of limit.

Achilles can run ten times as fast as the tortoise. If the tortoise is given 100m start when Achilles runs that 100m, the tortoise is at 110m, then at 111m when Achilles is at 110m, and so on. Thus the tortoise will always be one tenth further on infinitely.

acre An imperial unit of area measure. There are 2.47 acres to 1 **hectare**.

Q How many acres in 3ha?
A 3 × 2.47 = 7.41, thus there are approximately 7.41 acres in 3ha.

acting out a problem A process where a model or another representation can be used to enable the problem solver to gain a greater understanding of the problem. Using paper disks to model a far bigger **Tower of Hanoi** problem.

acute-angle An angle greater than 0° and less than 90°.

acute-angled triangle A triangle where all 3 angles are acute.
In general *a*, *b*, *c* are all less than 90°.

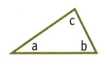

Excel Junior High School Maths Study Dictionary

A accumulated

accumulated Collecting together.
The accumulated investments of the company were $125 000.

AD, anno domini Latin meaning *in the year of our Lord*. Indicates calendar years after the birth of Christ. *Sydney held the Olympics in 2000AD*

add The process of **addition**. To combine together.
Q Add 2 and 4
A This means:
```
  2
+ 4
———
  6
```

addend Any of the numbers being added. Both 2 and 5 are addends.
2   +   5   =   7
addend + addend = sum

addition The process of combining two or more numbers. Also called the **sum**. Opposite to **subtraction**.

of decimals: Place the decimal points under each other. Include zero(s) to fill gaps.

Q Add 4.2 and 3.71
A Use the vertical algorithm
```
  4.20 including the 0
+ 3.71
——————
  7.91
```

of directed numbers: Combine the two signed numbers.

Q Find: −2 + 3
A −2 + 3 = +1

Adding a negative number is the same as subtracting a positive number.

Q Find −3 + −4
A −3 + −4 becomes −3 − 4 = −7

addition property of zero

of fractions: First express each separate fraction with the same (lowest common) denominator and then add the resultant numerators.

Q Find $\frac{2}{3} + \frac{3}{4}$

A $\frac{2}{3} + \frac{3}{4} = \frac{2 \times 4 + 3 \times 3}{12} = \frac{8 + 9}{12} = \frac{17}{12} = 1\frac{5}{12}$, after simplifying.

of fractions in algebra: Use the same process as for numeric fractions.

Q Find $\frac{2a}{3} + \frac{3a}{4}$

A $\frac{2a}{3} + \frac{3a}{4} = \frac{2a \times 4 + 3a \times 3}{12} = \frac{8a + 9a}{12} = \frac{17a}{12}$

Note: The result is left as an **improper fraction**. A mixed number makes no sense.

of mixed numbers: Add the whole numbers and then add the fractions.

Q Add $2\frac{1}{3}$ and $1\frac{2}{5}$.

A $2\frac{1}{3} + 1\frac{2}{5} = 2 + 1 + \frac{1}{3} + \frac{2}{5} = 3 + \frac{5 + 6}{15} = 3\frac{11}{15}$

of surds: Surds can only be added if they are the same.

Q Find $\sqrt{3} + 2\sqrt{3} + \sqrt{5}$

A Only the $\sqrt{3}$s can be added. Thus $\sqrt{3} + 2\sqrt{3} + \sqrt{5} = 3\sqrt{3} + \sqrt{5}$

of whole numbers:

Q Add 34 and 47
A Use the vertical algorithm
```
  34
+ 47
----
  81
```

addition property of zero When zero is added to any number the (result) sum is the same as the original number.

$7 + 0 = 7$ and also $0 + 7 = 7$

Excel Junior High School Maths Study Dictionary

A additive inverse

additive inverse The opposite. The value which gives **zero** when added to the original number.

> **Q** Find the additive inverse of −6.
> **A** 6 and −6 are additive inverses because:
> 6 + −6 = 0 and −6 + 6 = 0.

adjacent Next to.
AB and AC are adjacent sides in the figure.

adjacent angles Two angles that have a common arm and a common vertex. The other arms lie on either side of the common arm.
$A\hat{B}C$ and $C\hat{B}D$ are adjacent
common vertex B
common arm BC

adjacent faces Two faces in a shape are adjacent if they meet at a common edge.

Adjacent faces

adjacent side The side next to the angle in a right-angled triangle that is not the **hypotenuse**. Used in **trigonometry**.

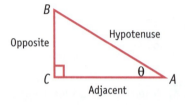

AC is the side adjacent to the angle θ (= $B\hat{A}C$).

aeon 10^9 years

1 000 000 000 years.

algebra The use of letters (**variables** or **pronumerals**) or similar symbols (such as **Greek** letters) with numbers to show a relationship. A significant use is to create **equations**. Derived from an Arabic word *Al-jabr*.

$2x + 3 = 5,\quad 3x^2 - 7x + 9,\quad \Delta + \Delta + \Delta = 3\Delta$

algebraic addition Only like terms (terms that use exactly the same variable or symbol) can be added.
Note: *ab* and *ba* are like terms while *x* and x^2 are unlike terms.

> Q Find: $2a + 3a$, $2ab + 3ba$, $3x + 2x^2$
> A $2a + 3a = 5a$,
> $2ab + 3ba = 2ab + 3ab = 5ab$
> However $3x + 2x^2 = 3x + 2x^2$ as the terms *x* and x^2 are not like terms.

algebraic equation See **equations**.

algebraic expression See **expression, algebraic**.

algebraic fractions Obey the same rules as numeric fractions.
addition: A common denominator is first found for addition.

> Q Simplify $\dfrac{2}{a+1} + \dfrac{3}{a-1}$
> A $\dfrac{2}{a+1} + \dfrac{3}{a-1} = \dfrac{2(a-1) + 3(a+1)}{(a+1)(a-1)}$
> $\phantom{\dfrac{2}{a+1} + \dfrac{3}{a-1}} = \dfrac{5a + 1}{(a+1)(a-1)}$

subtraction: A common denominator is first found for subtraction.

> Q Simplify $\dfrac{2}{5x} - \dfrac{3}{2y}$
> A $\dfrac{2}{5x} - \dfrac{3}{2y} = \dfrac{2 \times 2y - 3 \times 5x}{5x \times 2y} = \dfrac{4y - 15x}{10xy}$

algebraic subtraction

multiplication: Takes advantage of cancelling first.

Q Simplify $\dfrac{9a^2}{2x} \times \dfrac{xy}{3a}$

A $\dfrac{^3\cancel{9}a^2}{2\cancel{x}_1} \times \dfrac{^1\cancel{x}y}{3_1\cancel{a}} = \dfrac{3ay}{2}$

division: Takes advantage of cancelling after the process of inversion and multiplication is first applied.

Q Complete $\dfrac{xy}{z} \div \dfrac{y}{z^2}$

A $\dfrac{xy}{z} \div \dfrac{y}{z^2} = \dfrac{x\cancel{y}^1}{\cancel{z}_1} \times \dfrac{\cancel{z}^2}{\cancel{y}_1} = xz$

algebraic subtraction   Only like terms (terms that use exactly the same variable or symbol) can be subtracted. Note: *ab* and *ba* are like terms while *x* and x^2 are unlike terms.

Q Find: $5a - 3a$, $8ab - 3ba$, $3x - 2x^2$
A $5a - 3a = 2a$, $8ab - 3ba = 8ab - 3ab = 5ab$
However $3x - 2x^2 = 3x - 2x^2$ as the terms *x* and x^2 are not like terms.

algebraic inequality   See **inequality**.

algebraic term   See **term**.

algorism   See **algorithm**.

algorithm   A rule (routine) to solve a problem in a number of steps. From a Latin translation of the name of an Arabic scholar *al-Khwarizmi*. See also **algebra**, previous page.

Q Find the sum of 23 and 39.
A $\begin{array}{r} 23 \\ +39 \\ \hline 62 \end{array}$ is the algorithm.

allied angles See co-interior angles.

alpha, α The first letter of the Greek alphabet. Often used as a variable or unknown.
   Find the value of the angle α.

alphanumeric data Data consisting of letters and numbers, or letters only.

alternate angles Usually associated with parallel lines. When parallel lines are cut by a transversal, two pairs of equal alternate angles are formed.

Note: Any two non-parallel lines when cut by a transversal display unequal alternate angles.

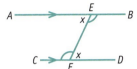

altitude Height or perpendicular distance.

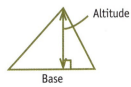

am See ante meridiem.

amount How much.
   Q What is the amount when $2.50 is multiplied by 4?
   A As 2.50 × 4 = 10, the amount is $10.00.

A  analog(ue)

analog(ue) Measuring devices that use physical quantities rather than digits. Quantities are shown on a **scale**, such as time on a clock face or cm on a ruler.

Q Show five minutes past 3 o'clock.
A

Q Measure this length.

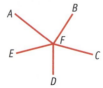

A The line is 24 mm.

angle A measure of the amount of turn from one line to another about a common point. Also the shape formed when two lines (or rays) intersect. The two lines are called the **arms** of the angle and the intersection the **vertex**.
at a point: Where two or more lines meet at a point to make several angles. The sum of all of these angles is 360°.

allied: see **co-interior angles**.
alternate: see **alternate angles**, previous page.
complementary: see **complementary angles**.
corresponding: see **corresponding angles**.
name: The angle shown can be named $A\hat{B}C$ or $\angle ABC$ or A.

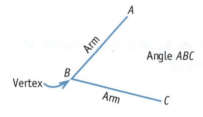

Angle ABC

continued over

angle

obtuse: see **obtuse angle**.
reflex: see **reflex angle**.
straight: see **straight angle**.
supplementary: see **supplementary angles**.
vertically opposite: see **vertically opposite angles**.

angle
of depression: see **depression**.
of elevation: see **elevation**.
of inclination: see **elevation**.

angle properties of the circle
See **circle, angle properties**.

angle sum
of polygon: Given by the formula $q = (n - 2) \times 180°$, where n is the number of sides of the polygon.

> **Q** Find the angle sum of a hexagon.
> **A** A hexagon has 6 sides, thus the sum is $(6 - 2) \times 180° = 4 \times 180° = 720°$

of quadrilateral: Equal to 360° or 4 right angles. The formula gives $(4 - 2) \times 180° = 2 \times 180 = 360°$.

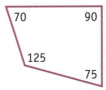

of triangle: Equal to 180° or 2 right angles. The formula gives $(3 - 2) \times 180° = 1 \times 180 = 180°$.

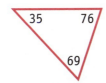

Excel Junior High School Maths Study Dictionary

A angles of a complete revolution

angles of a complete revolution Angles about a point that share a common *vertex* and add together to give a total of 360°.

angular distance The angular difference between two directions (or bearings) giving the angle between the two directions. See also *bearings* and *surveyors' bearings*.

annual (annually) A once a year happening or event.
The Fair is an annual event.
The annual increase in production was 7%.

annulus The area generated between two *concentric circles*.

ante meridiem (am) Before midday (noon). From Latin. The opposite to *post meridiem (pm)*; after midday. Times from after midnight to noon.
Note: Noon is not an am or pm time.

6 am is 6 hours after midnight.

anti-clockwise Turning in the opposite direction to the movement of the hands of an *analog* clock. Also called counter-clockwise.

antiparallel lines

antiparallel lines Cut any pair of lines to form equal angles in *opposite order*.

apex 1. The pointy end of a cone or the **vertex** opposite the base of a triangle.
2. The highest point relative to a base line.

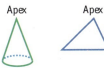

apex angle The angle at the top of a triangle.

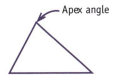

apothem The **perpendicular** in a regular **polygon** from its centre to one of the sides and so bisects the side.

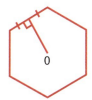 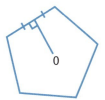

application The use of a theoretical result to solve a problem.
of algebraic equations: To rewrite problems written in words into algebraic sentences (equations).

Q **The product of a number and 8 is 56. What is the number?**
A Let the number be *n*. $8 \times n = 56$ $\therefore n = 7$
Thus the number is 7.

approximate

of decimals: Use the decimal equivalent. For example 100 m = 0.1 km, or 23% = 0.23. Then multiply by the decimal to obtain the result.

Q Find 0.17 of 800 m.
A 800 m × 0.17 = 136.   0.17 of 800 m is 136 m.

of fractions:

Q Find $\frac{3}{4}$ of 480 g.
A $\frac{3}{4}$ × 480 = 360. $\frac{3}{4}$ of 480 g = 360 g.

of percentages:

Q Find 15.6% of $500.
A 500 × 15.6 ÷ 100 = 78.   15.6% of $500 = $78.

approximate To obtain a value to a particular **accuracy**. For example, 3.14 is an approximation to π, correct to two decimal places.

approximately A close estimate of an amount or total. Found by rounding. See **rounding**.

Q Give 1 200 456 as a decimal of millions.
A 1 200 456 is approximately 1.2 million.

approximation(s) Rounding off. The symbols ≈ ≃ ≐ are used. See **rounding**.

To round off (or approximate) correct to a given number, we round up if the next digit is 5 or more and round down if the next digit is less than 5. 326 is approximately 330 and 324 is approximately 320.

arabic numerals The digits 0, 1, 2, 3, 4, 5, 6, 7, 8, 9 more commonly (and correctly) called the **Hindu-Arabic numerals**.

arbelos The region bounded by three semicircles.

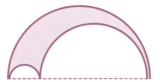

arbitrary unit Any measuring device that is not a standard unit of measurement. Some examples:

Hand span

24 buckets full

arbitrary (free) variable A variable whose scope is not limited by a logical quantifier. Free variables are frequently used in proofs to represent an arbitrary element of a set. See also variable, arbitrary.

arc Part of the circumference of a circle.

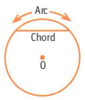

archimedean spiral A spiral drawn where the radius increases proportionally to the angle through which it has turned.

$r = k\theta$, where k is a number (constant)

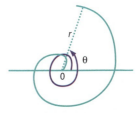

A archimedes' principle

archimedes' principle See **displacement (2)**.

are Metric unit of area that is 10 m × 10 m.

1 are = 100 m² | 10 m × 10 m

area The amount or size of a surface, the amount of space inside a **two-dimensional (2D)** shape, measured in square units.

area of

triangle (1):

$$A = \frac{1}{2}bh$$

parallelogram:

$$A = bh$$

Note: The base is not necessarily on the bottom.

Q Find the area of:

A $A = \frac{1}{2} \times 9 \times 7$
   $= 31.5 \text{ cm}^2$

Q Find the area of:

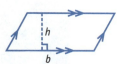

A $A = 13 \times 8$
   $= 104 \text{ m}^2$

quadrilateral:
Divide into 2 triangles.

$$A = \frac{1}{2}dh_1 + \frac{1}{2}dh_2$$
$$= \frac{1}{2}d(h_1 + h_2)$$

rectangle:
Width and breadth mean the same.

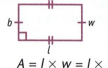

$$A = l \times w = l \times b$$

area of

Q Find the area of:

A $A = \frac{1}{2} \times 15 \times (6 + 9)$

  $= 112.5 \text{ m}^2$

Q Find the area of:

A $A = 12 \times 8$

  $= 96 \text{ m}^2$

rhombus and kite:

$A = \frac{1}{2}xy$

trapezium:

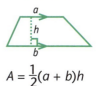

$A = \frac{1}{2}(a + b)h$

Q Find the area of:

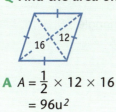

A $A = \frac{1}{2} \times 12 \times 16$

  $= 96 \text{ u}^2$

Q Find the area of:

A $A = \frac{11 + 17}{2} \times 9$

  $= 14 \times 9$

  $= 126 \text{ m}^2$

of triangle (2): The area can be found using **trigonometry**.

Area $= \frac{1}{2}ab \sin C$

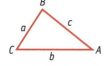

Q Find the area of triangle *XYZ*.

A $A = \frac{1}{2} \times 17 \times 13 \times \sin 25° = 46.7 \text{ cm}^2$ (correct to 1 decimal place)

continued over

A area of

of shaded figures: The area can be found by subtraction.

Q Find the shaded area.

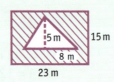

A $A = 23 \times 15 - \frac{1}{2} \times 8 \times 5 = 345 - 20$
$= 325 \text{ m}^2$

of composite figures: The area can be found by adding the areas of the component parts.

Q Find the area of the figure:

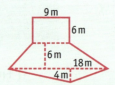

A The figure consists of a rectangle, a trapezium and a triangle.
$A = 9 \times 6 + \frac{(9+18)}{2} \times 6 + \frac{1}{2} \times 18 \times 4$
$= 54 + 81 + 36$
$= 171 \text{ m}^2$

of circles: $A = \pi r^2$, where r is the radius of the circle.

Q Find the area of the circle.

A $A = \pi r^2$
$= \pi \times 3^2$
$= 9\pi \text{ u}^2$

of sectors: $A = \pi r^2 \frac{\theta}{360}$

Q Find the area of a sector subtended by an angle of 72° in a circle of radius 6 cm.

A $A = \pi \times 6^2 \times \frac{72}{360} = 22.62 \text{ cm}^2$ (to 2 decimal places)

arithmetic A

arithmetic The part of mathematics that uses numbers and their operations. Contrast with **algebra**. The addition, subtraction, multiplication and division of **whole numbers**, **decimals** and **fractions** and calculation of **percentages**.

arithmetic mean The result of dividing the sum of a set of numbers by the count of the numbers.
For the numbers 1, 3, 6, 8, 10; the mean is
$\bar{x} = \frac{1 + 3 + 6 + 8 + 10}{5} = 5.6 = 5\frac{3}{5}$. The symbol $\bar{x}$ represents the arithmetic mean, (average or mean).
Note: The division is by 5 because there are 5 numbers in the set.

arithmetic sequence (progression) Equally spaced numbers. Each number is found by the addition of a common difference.
Example: 1, 4, 7, 10, 13, 16, . . . has a common difference of 3 (7 − 4 = 4 − 1 = 3).

arithmetic series The sum of an arithmetic sequence.
1 + 4 + 7 + 10 + 13 + 16 + . . .

arms The two sides of an angle. The **rays** or lines that form an **angle**. See these entries also.

array A rectangular arrangement of numbers or other symbols. Often used in probability. Also known as a **lattice diagram**. See **dot diagram** also.

1	2	3
2	4	5
3	5	6

Excel Junior High School Maths Study Dictionary

A arrow

arrow Used to show parallel lines and to indicate continuation of a line.

To show different pair of parallel lines

Number line

ascending order Where each number is larger than the one before.

2, 2.3, $2\frac{1}{2}$, 2.6, . . .   Thus $2 < 2.3 < 2\frac{1}{2} < 2.6$

of decimals:

Q Write in ascending order: 2.1, 2.01, 2.11, 2.001, 2
A 2, 2.001, 2.01, 2.1, 2.11

of directed numbers:

Q Write in ascending order: 3, −4, +2, 0, −1.
A Unsigned values are given + signs.
−4, −1, 0, +2, +3

of fractions:

Q Write in ascending order: $2\frac{1}{2}$, 2, $2\frac{1}{4}$, $2\frac{1}{3}$.

A 2, $2\frac{1}{4}$, $2\frac{1}{3}$, $2\frac{1}{2}$

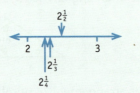

askew Oblique or awry. As opposed to a perpendicular line.

association The relationship between the two sets of variables in a scatter diagram. The possible associations are positive, negative or none. See **scatter diagram**.

associative law See **associative property**, below.

associative property The property for addition and multiplication where the order of the operation makes no difference to the answer. Note: Subtraction and division are not associative.
  addition example: $(2 + 6) + 4 = 2 + (6 + 4)$
  multiplication example: $(2 \times 6) \times 4 = 2 \times (6 \times 4)$

assumption Something that is accepted to be true without proof. At the very basis of almost any problem is the need to make behavioural assumptions about key values.
Example: In a modelling situation about seating a suitable assumption would be that no person is more than 60 cm wide.

astronomical unit The mean distance from the centre of the Earth to the centre of the Sun. Approximately 150 000 000 km.

astroid The curve traced out by a point on the **circumference** of a circle rolling on the inside of a circle that is four times its **radius**.

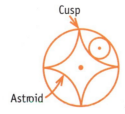

A asymmetric

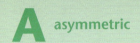

asymmetric A figure without symmetry. The figure is irregular.

No axis of symmetry

asymptotes A line representing the value that a graph approaches but can never touch. A limit of the graph.

Asymptotes

attometre The shortest unit of length 1×10^{-18} m = 1am.

attribute A characteristic of an object, such as size, colour, shape or thickness. See **data** also.

Triangle

Thin

Thick

average More correctly called the mean or **arithmetic mean**. See this entry.

average Rate The average (or mean) of two or more rates. Not constant at all times. See also **uniform rate** and **rate**.

10 km/h 18 km/h
15 min 10 min

The average rate for the journey is:

$$\frac{\frac{10}{4} + \frac{18}{6}}{\frac{25}{60}} = 13.2 \text{ km/h}$$

The calculation requires division of each rate by the part of the hour travelled (15 minutes is one-quarter and 10 minutes is one-sixth) and then division of the sum by the fraction of the hour for the total journey.

Avogadro's number The name Avogadro's number is just an *honorary name* attached to the calculated value of the number of atoms, molecules, etc. in a gram mole (**SI** base unit) of any chemical substance. The value is 6.0225×10^{23}.

award rate The rate of payment agreed to by arbitration or workplace agreement.

axes Plural of **axis**.
1 Multiple lines along which **coordinates** can be measured.

 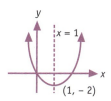

2 The lines used as a reference in graphs.

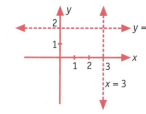

axiom A statement accepted to be true without proof. Forms the basis from which other statements and proofs (**theorems**) are developed.
Euclid: 'If equals are added to equals the results are equal'.

axis Can refer to a **graph** or a physical property. Also 'the Earth spins on its axis'.

axis of symmetry A line that divides a figure into two identical parts that are mirror images of each other. Also called the **line of symmetry**.

 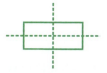

B b

B b

1 The capital letter B and other letters are used in diagrams to name points, lines and angles.

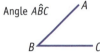
Angle $A\hat{B}C$

Side b is opposite angle B

2 The lower case letter b and other letters are used as **variables** in **algebra**.

Q If $3a + 7b = 10$, if $a = 1$, find the value of b. Note $1b$ is written as b.
A $3 × 1 + 7b = 10$, gives $3 - 3 + 7b = 10 - 3$ and then $7b = 7$ ∴ $b = 1$

back-to-back Showing two values or two relationships next to each other. An example is with a back-to-back **stem-and-leaf-plot**.

```
5 3 1 1 |2| 2 5 7
    7 2 1 |3| 1 3 5 7
  7 7 3 2 |4| 2 2 4 5 7
```

backtracking A method of solving equations by reversing the steps that created the **equation**.

Q Solve $3x - 2 = 8$ by backtracking.
A First step: remove any other terms by using the reverse operation (+2)
$3x - 2 + 2 = 8 + 2$
Thus $3x = 10$
Second step: remove the multiplier by division.
$\frac{3x}{3} = \frac{10}{3}$
∴ $x = 3\frac{1}{3}$

balance **1** To maintain or retain **equilibrium**. When completing the square, add the square to both sides of the equation to maintain its balance.
2 Remaining sum of money or debt after a calculation or transaction. After deducting the payment the balance on the loan was $23 467.

bar A line above a letter or symbol used to give it a special meaning.

Recurring decimal $\frac{1}{3} = 0.\overline{3}$ 　　　More usually written with a dot: $\frac{1}{3} = 0.\dot{3}$

Repeating decimal $\frac{1}{7} = 0.\overline{142857}$

Mean (average)　$\bar{x}$

Roman numerals: $\bar{C}$ is 1000 times C, thus $\bar{\bar{C}}$ = 100 000 and similarly $\bar{V}$ = 5000, $\bar{X}$ = 10 000, $\bar{L}$ = 50 000, $\bar{D}$ = 500 000. $\bar{M}$ = 1 000 000.

bar graph (chart) Values are shown as separated horizontal rectangles.
Note: There are inconsistent uses of the terms bar and column for graphs. Also called a horizontal bar graph. See also **column graph**.

bar graph, divided Used to show percentages of a quantity or amount through the use of a rectangle. Also called a compound bar graph.

base

1 A face of a solid, which gives the name of the **prism** or **pyramid**.

Rectangular pyramid

2 One side of a triangle used in the area formula $A = \frac{1}{2} b.h$

3 The number on which a counting system is constructed.
1, 2, 10, 11, 12, 20, 21, 22, 100, . . . is using 3 as the base.

4 The number that is raised to a **power**. For $2^3 = 8$, 2 is the base.

B base line

base line The horizontal or *x-axis* of a graph.

base ten numeration Our system of counting based on 10 digits and place value. Also called the **Hindu-Arabic** system.
1 2 3 4 5 6 7 8 9 0

basic numeral The simplest answer to a computation.

Q **Give 20 − 4 + 8 − 2 as its basic numeral**
A 20 − 4 + 8 − 2 = 16 + 8 − 2
             = 24 − 2
             = 22

battleships A game using the idea of plotting **coordinates**. Each player secretly places five ships on a 10 × 10 grid and then the players take turns at trying to locate the ships by giving a coordinate pair as a possible location.

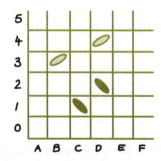

BC Before Christ. Used to indicate years in the ancient calendar.
Caesar landed in the British Isles in 55BC.

bearing The angle used to show direction as a clockwise turn from the North direction. Also called compass bearing. See also **surveyors' bearings** and **true bearings**.

NE is 45° clockwise from N

bi A prefix meaning two. See **bimodal**.
A bicycle has two wheels.

bias A tendency to favour one side rather than acting straight down the middle. Used in **statistics** to indicate that a sample of the population is not truly representative.
A common use of bias is in lawn bowls where one side of the bowl is shaved thus making the bowl turn towards the other side.

bicentenary Two centuries. A happening after two hundred years.
The bicentenary of white settlement in Australia occurred in 1988.

billion Now considered to be 1000 million (= 10^9) as used in the USA. The UK still uses one million million (= 10^{12})
1 000 000 000 is 1 billion in Australia.

B bimodal

bimodal Data having two modes. See also **mode**.

> **Q** Give the mode(s) of: 1, 2, 2, 2, 3, 5, 6, 6, 6, 7, 9
> **A** The set has 2 and 6 as modes (both occurring most, 3 times) and so is bimodal.

binary numbers The counting system that uses 1 and 0 only. The machine language of computers is based on binary code.

binary operation A process that combines two numbers into a third number. Addition (+), subtraction (−), multiplication (×) and division (÷) are examples. $2 + 3 = 5$ is an example of a closed binary operation.

binomial expression Used in **algebra**. An expression that contains two terms as an addition or subtraction.
$a + b$ and $3x − 2y$ are both binomial expressions.

binomial products The multiplication of two binomial expressions. $(a + b)(c + d)$ is an example of a binomial product.

bisect To cut, or divide, into two equal parts. Usually refers to an **angle** or an **interval**.

bisector The line that carries out a bisection. See the diagram above.

bit Abbreviation for **bi**nary digit. Used in binary numbers especially in machine code in calculators and computers.
0 and 1 are examples.

bivariate data See **data, bivariate**.

bonus Payment above the normal or contracted amount for services rendered. Usually an incentive payment.

book value The depreciated value of a capital item in a company's assets. The depreciated value of the original purchase price. It is not necessarily the market value. See also **depreciation**.

boundary 1 A border or curve around a region.

PQRST is the boundary of the pentagon.
BCAO encloses the region shaded.

2 The number where an inequality begins or ends. Indicated on the number line by an open or closed circle. See **inequality**.

box-and-whiskers diagram Use in statistics to show spread or distribution of a set of data. See also **modern box plot**.

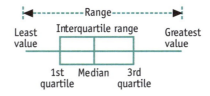

B box-and-whiskers diagram

Q Show the data 1, 2, 3, 3, 4, 6, 6, 6, 7, 9, 10, 13, 14 as a box-and-whiskers diagram.

A

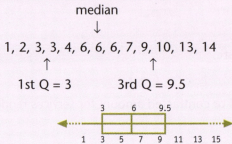

box plot See above for box-and-whiskers diagram.

braces A grouping symbol. Sometimes called 'wriggly brackets' { }. See **brackets**.

brackets 1 The collective term often used for most grouping symbols. There are three main types of brackets. Their proper names are **braces** { }, brackets [ ] and **parentheses** ( ). When used together they usually appear nested as follows. {[( )]}.
2 A grouping symbol. Often called 'square brackets'.
[ ]. See also **grouping symbols**.

breadth The distance from one side of a figure to another. Another name for width.

Bridges of Königsberg A famous network problem that formed part of the basis of topology.

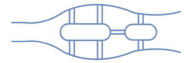

broken line See dotted line.

budget A plan for using money. A projected expense account and records of spending on items. Used in consumer arithmetic.

Rent	$140
Food	$60
Clothing	$40
Entertainment	$50
Travel	$40
Total	$330

byte A unit of information in computing, usually equivalent to a single character.

1 or 0

C c

C 1 The symbol that is used to show the Celsius temperature scale. See **Celsius**.
2 The symbol for the **circumference** of a circle:

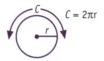

3 The capital letter C and other letters are used in **diagrams** to name **points**, lines and angles.

4 The lower case letter c and other letters are used as **variables** in **algebra**.

> **Q** If $3a + 6c = 15$, if $a = 1$, find the value of c.
> **A** $3 \times 1 + 6c = 15$ which gives $6c = 12$ and thus $c = 2$

Note: $1c$ is written as c.

calculate Carry out addition +, subtraction −, multiplication × or division ÷, together with powers or roots of numbers, or a combination of these operations to get an answer. Then separately write the answer so that the marker can clearly see it. Note: *You should not expect the marker to go looking for your answer!*

calculator use The different calculators have most functions in common. There are some differences however. Each new model has features that change. You need to read the calculator handbook to find out how to use all the functions.
and directed numbers: Generally the negative sign followed by a number and then a power gives a negative result.

> **Q** Find -2^2
> **A** Enter ⊖ 2 x^2 = to get -4

The ⊖ button on a *Casio fx82AU* or the ± button on the *Sharp* and some other Casio models changes the sign.

calculator use

[−] 3 [×] [−] 3 gives (−3) × (−3) = 9 *(Casio)* and
either [±] 3 [×] [±] 3 [=] or 3 [±] [×] 3 [±] [=] gives (−3) × (−3) = 9 *(Sharp)*.

Q Find $(-2)^2$
A Enter [−] 2 [x^2] *(Casio)* or 2 [±] [x^2] *(Sharp)* to obtain 4.
Note: $(-)2^2 = -4$ *(Casio)* and $\pm 2x^2 = -4$ *(Sharp)*.

and fractions: Use the [$a^b/_c$] button to enter fractions and mixed numbers.

Q Add $2\frac{2}{3}$ and $3\frac{3}{4}$.
A Enter 2 [$a^b/_c$] 2 [$a^b/_c$] 3 + 3 [$a^b/_c$] 3 [$a^b/_c$] 4 = to give 6⌐5⌐12 *(Casio)* or
2 [$a^b/_c$] 2 [$a^b/_c$] 3 + 3 [$a^b/_c$] 3 [$a^b/_c$] 4 = to give 6r5r12 *(Sharp)*.
Answer is $6\frac{5}{12}$

to convert mixed numbers to improper fractions and return.

Q1 Convert $2\frac{2}{3}$ to an improper fraction.
A Enter 2 [$a^b/_c$] 2 [$a^b/_c$] 3 = [SHIFT] [$a^b/_c$] to give 8⌐3 *(Casio)* or
2 [$a^b/_c$] 2 [$a^b/_c$] 3 = [SHIFT] [$a^b/_c$] to give 8r3 *(Sharp)*.
Answer is $\frac{8}{3}$

Q2 Convert $\frac{8}{3}$ to a mixed number.
A Enter 8 [$a^b/_c$] 3 = to give 2⌐2⌐3 *(Casio)* or
2 [$a^b/_c$] 2 [$a^b/_c$] 3 = [2ndF] [$a^b/_c$] to give 2r2r3 *(Sharp)*.
Answer is $2\frac{2}{3}$

and percentages: First convert the percentage to a decimal by dividing by 100.

Q Find 20% of $560
A 20 [÷] 100 [×] 560 [=] 112

and powers: [x^2] gives a square while [y^x] *Sharp* and [x^y] *Casio* gives higher powers.

Q Find 4^3
A Enter 4 [x^y] 3 *Casio* or 4 [y^x] 3 *Sharp* to get 64.

continued over

and roots: $\sqrt{}$ gives square root, $\sqrt[3]{}$ cube root and $\sqrt[x]{}$ higher roots.

Q Find $\sqrt[5]{32}$

A Enter 5 [SHIFT] [x^y] 32 [=] *Casio* or 5 [2ndF] [y^x] 32 [=] *Sharp* to get 2.

and scientific notation: Use the 10^x button.

Q Find $7 \times 4.3 \times 10^3$

A Enter 7×4.3 [×] [SHIFT] [log] 3 [=] *Casio* or $7 \times 4.3 \times$ [2ndF] [log] 3 [=] *Sharp* to get 30100.

calendar The calendar in almost universal use has evolved over many centuries. It is based on earlier measurements of the seasons by ancient peoples such as the Babylonians, Egyptians and Mayans. There are 365 days in a normal year and 366 days in a **leap year**.

calliper A clamp-like measuring device for measuring small distances such as external or internal diameters. The dividers supplied in a set of geometrical instruments is another example.

cancelling Common name for the process of simplification usually associated with fractions. It involves division of a **numerator** and a **denominator** by a **common factor**.

$\dfrac{\cancel{9}^3}{\cancel{12}^4} = \dfrac{3}{4}$ (divide by 3) and

$\dfrac{\cancel{8}^2}{\cancel{15}^3} \times \dfrac{\cancel{5}^1}{\cancel{12}^3} = \dfrac{2 \times 1}{3 \times 3} = \dfrac{2}{9}$ (divide by 4 and 5).

c-angles Alternative name for co-interior angles. See this entry.

capacity The amount of liquid or gas that a container can hold. It is measured in litres.
and volume: The volume of a solid is equivalent to its capacity. $1 \text{ cm}^3 = 1 \text{ mL}$
units: 1000 mL = 1 L   1000 L = 1 kL
1000 kL = 1 000 000 L = 1 ML (megalitre)

cardinal numbers The number of elements in a set. The number name given to the last member of the set counted.

Example: For a normal deck of cards, the cardinal number is 52 as there are 52 cards in the deck. See cards.

cardioid A heart shaped figure (thus the name) generated by drawing circles centred at regular intervals on the circumference of a circle, all passing through a fixed point on the circle. There are other ways to produce the figure.

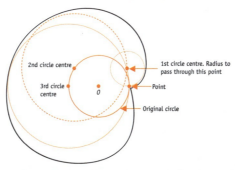

cards, standard pack

cards, standard pack The standard pack of cards contains 52 cards in 4 suits (hearts, diamonds, clubs and spades). The cards in each suit are Ace, King, Queen, Jack, 10 to 2. The Court cards are King, Queen and Jack.

Carroll diagram A method of recording classification. Used by Mathematician Charles Lutwiger Dodgson, 1832-1898, better known as Lewis Carroll, the author of *Alice in Wonderland*.

carrying The process of regrouping when adding or multiplying when the result is greater than 9.

```
   1            2
  25           23
 + 7          × 7
 ----         ----
  32          161
```

Cartesian coordinates Named after Rene Descartes, the French philosopher and mathematician, 1596-1650, the developer of the system of positioning on the number plane with a number pair (x, y). See **coordinates**.

casual work A form of employment. Usually paid at an hourly or daily rate where a rate higher than the permanent wage is paid to allow for no holiday or sick pay. See **wage** and **salary**.

categorical data

categorical data Data (information) that can be classified according to a category. This data can be nominal or ordinal. See also **nominal data** and **ordinal data**.

Pet	Number
cat	4
dog	7
bird	5
other	3

The pets are placed in categories. The numbers show how many of each category.

cc A now obsolete form for cubic centimetres (cm^3). Usually associated with engine capacity in motor vehicles, from a method of taxing motor vehicles in Great Britain.

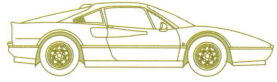

Is the engine capacity 3280ccs? No it is 3.28L

Celsius scale The **metric system** temperature scale that gives the melting point of ice as zero degrees and the boiling point of water as 100 degrees. Used almost universally, apart from the USA. Named after the Swedish astronomer Anders Celsius, 1701-1744.

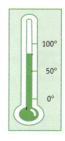

census The method of data collection that examines every member of the population.
The Australian government conducts a national census every 5 years where information is gathered about every citizen.

cent

cent The smallest unit of Australian currency. One hundredth part of a dollar. Now only used in electronic commerce. The smallest coin in circulation is the 5 cent coin.

centi A prefix meaning one hundredth. Used in measurement units.
Length: *centimetre* Mass: *centigram* Capacity: *centilitre*

centigrade A now rarely used name for the **Celsius** temperature scale.

centimetre One hundredth part of a metre.

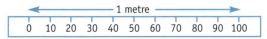

central tendency The tendency for **data** to collect about the middle point in the data. See separate entries for **mean**, **median** and **mode**.

centre For a circle. The point that defines a circle as a point moving so that it is a constant distance from a fixed point. See **circle**.

centre of rotation (centre of symmetry) For **rotational symmetry**. The point about which the object rotates to display the symmetry.

Order 4 rotational symmetry

Order 3 rotational symmetry

Excel Junior High School Maths Study Dictionary

certain   Used in probability to indicate the likelihood of an event that must happen. The probability of a certain event is 1. The opposite to the impossible event.
It is certain that the sun will set tonight.

centroid of a triangle   The point of intersection of the medians of a triangle. For a triangular plane shape this is the point of balance of the triangle.

century   One hundred.
The 20th Century ran from 1901 to 2000.
The batsman scored 200 runs, a double century.

chain   An imperial measure of length. The length of a cricket pitch, stump to stump.

chance (probability)   The likelihood of an event.
addition principle: For mutually exclusive events the probability of A or B is the sum of the separate probabilities.   Pr(A or B) = Pr(A) + Pr(B)
compound events: A combining of two separate events.

Q Give all the possible outcomes when a coin is tossed and a die is then rolled.
A   1   2   3   4   5   6
Head   H1   H2   H3   H4   H5   H6
Tail   T1   T2   T3   T4   T5   T6

These events are not related so the number of outcome is the product of the two separate chances. (2 × 6 =12)   *continued over*

chance, contingency table

chance, contingency table: A rectangular table that shows information for two variables, with one set of categories on the horizontal line and the other set on the vertical line. The information in the table is used to calculate probabilities. Similar to an array. Another name is a two-way-table.

Example: Boys, girls, men and women were asked to indicate their preference for a second colour in their newspaper. The data is shown below.

	boys	girls	men	women	total
red	9	11	6	7	33
blue	10	11	7	3	31
green	4	8	10	3	25
yellow	6	3	1	2	12
total	29	33	24	15	101

dependent events: Events where the outcome of one event will affect the outcome of the other.
Example: *Select two balls from a bag containing 5 red and 4 blue balls without replacement.*
The probability of the second selection depends on what is selected first.

dot diagrams: A method of showing outcomes. This is another form of an array. See these separate entries also.

dot plot: A vertical arrangement of a **dot diagram**. See above.

equally likely: Where two possible outcomes have the same theoretical probability.

chance, experimental probability

experimental probability: The number of times an event occurs compared with the total number of outcomes. See also theoretical probability (relative probability), next page. See also **probability** and **experimental probability**.

Equal to: $\Pr(\text{event}) = \dfrac{\text{frequency of score}}{\text{total frequency}} = \dfrac{f}{\Sigma f}$

> **Q** For the numbers 1, 1, 2, 4, 5, 6, 6, 6, 7, 8, 8 give Pr(6)
>
> **A** $\Pr(6) = \dfrac{3}{11}$

fair and unfair games: The rating of games of chance. A fair game is one where the operator and the player have an equal chance of winning while an unfair game is not. Two-up is considered a fair game as the odds of winning and losing are equal.

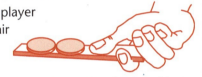

frequency tables: The frequency of a number of events can be displayed in a concise table. Calculation of **mean**, **median** and **mode** as well as **standard deviation** can be done using the table. Used for both grouped and ungrouped data.

> **Q** Use the frequency table to find the mean, median and mode:
>
> | Scores | 1 | 2 | 3 | 4 | 5 | 6 | 7 | 8 | 9 | 10 |
> |-----------|---|----|---|---|---|---|---|---|---|----|
> | Frequency | 9 | 11 | 6 | 7 | 3 | 5 | 8 | 9 | 4 | 2 |
>
> **A** See extra columns:
>
> | score (x) | no (f) | xf | cf |
> |-----------|--------|-----|----|
> | 1 | 9 | 9 | 9 |
> | 2 | 11 | 22 | 20 |
> | 3 | 6 | 18 | 26 |
> | 4 | 7 | 28 | 33 |
> | 5 | 3 | 15 | 36 |
> | 6 | 5 | 30 | 41 |
> | 7 | 8 | 56 | 49 |
> | 8 | 9 | 72 | 58 |
> | 9 | 4 | 36 | 62 |
> | 10 | 2 | 20 | 64 |
> | sum | 64 | 306 | |

continued over

chance, games of

Mean = 306/64 = 4.78 (to 2 decimal places)
Median: 64/2 = 32 (to find the centre score)
Thus median is 4 as 32nd and 33rd scores are both 4.
Mode is 2 as 11 is the largest frequency.

games of: The name given to games where chance influences the outcome. Cards, Monopoly and other dice games are examples. Money is often wagered on the result.

independent events: Events where the outcome of one event does not effect the outcome of the other.
Example is:
Select two balls from a bag containing 5 red and 4 blue balls with replacement.
This is because with replacement the contents of the bag is the same each time a ball is selected.

odds: The statement of a probability as a fraction, giving the amount that will be returned for a wager on a race or a game.
The odds of the favourite winning the Melbourne cup are 3 to 1.
Note: This implies there is one chance of winning to 3 chances of losing.

relative probability: For a large number of events, the proportion of successful trials to the total number of trials. See experimental probability, previous page. As the number of trials becomes very large, the relative probability approaches the **experimental probability**.

theoretical probability: The number of times the event can occur compared with the total number of possibilities. See also **experimental probability** and relative probability, above.

chance, diagrams

Equal to:
$$\Pr(\text{event}) = \frac{\text{number of times the event can occur}}{\text{total number of possibilities}}$$

Q For a standard six sided die give Pr(6).
A $\Pr(6) = \dfrac{\text{number of times the event can occur}}{\text{total number of possibilities}} = \dfrac{1}{6}$

tree diagrams: A diagram that displays all possible outcomes of an event in a systematic way.
Show the outcomes when a coin is tossed three times.

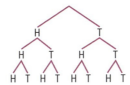

Venn diagrams: A display of elements in related sets using a rectangle and circles inside. Invented by the English logician John Venn in the eighteenth century.

Q Of 30 music students, 20 play the piano and 12 play the violin. How many play both?
A

The diagram shows an overlap of 2 students who play both.

chance event An event where the outcome is uncertain. A prediction of the possible outcome can be made using theoretical probability. See **probability**.

Q What is the chance of selecting the Ace from A, K, J, 9, 4?
A Chance = $\dfrac{1}{5}$

chance of success A measure of the likelihood of a successful outcome expressed as a fraction. See theoretical probability, on the previous page.

change In shopping. The amount you receive back when a larger amount is tendered.

> **Q** Find the change from $20 for a purchase of $14.71.
> **A** The change is 20 − 14.71 = 5.29 which would be $5.30 on rounding to the nearest 5c.

change the subject For a formula or equation. See **subject**.

check To try some value(s) to confirm that what is expected actually happens. The process used to make sure an answer is correct.

> **Q** Check that $3x + 2y = 5$ for $x = 1$ and $y = 1$.
> **A** LHS = $3 \times 1 + 2 \times 1 = 5$ = RHS

Chinese lattice Constructed from a hexagonal lattice with the centres of each pair of joined hexagons then joined by a straight line.

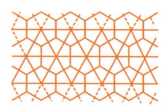

chord A straight line that joins two points on a curve, or a straight line drawn from one point on the **circumference** of a circle to another point on the circumference. The chord through the centre is the **diameter**. When a chord is extended it becomes a **secant**.

chord properties of a circle

chord properties of a circle

1 The angle between the tangent and the chord at the point of contact is equal to the angle in the alternate segment.

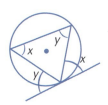

Q Find the angle *a*.

A $a = 70°$ (alternate segment)

2 a The line from the centre of a circle perpendicular to a chord bisects the chord.

Q If $AD = 7$ cm, find AB.

A As OD bisects AB, $AB = 2AD = 14$ cm.

b The perpendicular bisector of a chord passes through the centre of the circle.

c The line from the midpoint of a chord to the centre of the circle is perpendicular to the chord.

Q Find the length OD

A As angle ODB is a right angle use Pythagoras' theorem to find
$OD = \sqrt{7^2 - 6^2} = \sqrt{13}$ cm

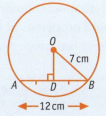

continued over

chord properties of a circle

3 Equal chords of a circle are the same distance from the centre and subtend equal angles at the centre.

Q Find the value of the pronumeral and give a reason.
A x is 45° as $AB = CD$.

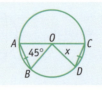

chronological order Placing events in historical order. The use of a **time line**.

circle The path of a point that moves so that it is a constant distance (the radius) from a fixed point (the centre).

area: Given by the formula $A = \pi r^2$, r, is the radius of the circle.

Q Find the area of the circle.
A $A = \pi r^2 = \pi \times 3^2 = 9\pi \, u^2$

and Pythagoras: Pythagoras' theorem is used with the right-angled triangles generated by the chord properties of the circle and the angle between the radius and the **tangent**. See **chord properties of a circle 2c**, on the previous page.

OTP is a right-angled triangle.

circle, angle properties

Q Find the value of x.

A Pythagoras' theorem gives $x^2 + 6^2 = 10^2$

Thus $x = \sqrt{100 - 36}$
$= \sqrt{64}$ cm
$= 8$ cm

angle properties:

1 The angle subtended at the centre is twice the angle at the circumference of a circle, standing on the same arc (or chord).

$2\, A\hat{C}B = A\hat{O}B$

on arc (chord) AB

Q Find the value of the pronumeral.

A $a = 2 \times 47° = 94°$

2 Angles at the circumference standing on the same or equal arc(s) (or chord) are equal.

$A\hat{C}B = A\hat{D}B$

AB common arc

$A\hat{E}B = C\hat{F}D$

equal chord $AB = CD$

Q Find the value of the pronumeral.

A $b = 43°$.

3 The angle in a **semicircle** is a right angle. This a special case of 1 where the angle at the centre is a straight angle.

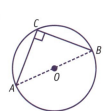

$A\hat{C}B = 90°$
as $A\hat{O}B = 180°$

circle, intersecting chords and secants

> **Q** Find the value of the pronumeral.
> **A** $e = 90°$ as *AOB* is a diameter.

diameter: The chord of a circle that passes through the centre.

intersecting chords and secants: The products of the intercepts of intersecting chords or secants are equal.

$AE \times EB = CE \times ED$ $AE \times EB = CE \times ED$

> **Q** Find the value of the pronumeral.
> **A** $(8 + 6) \times 6 = (x + 7) \times 7$
> $14 \times 6 \div 7 = x + 7$
> $12 = x + 7$
> $\therefore x = 5$

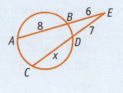

The square of the length of a tangent is equal to the product of the intercepts of a secant drawn from the external point.

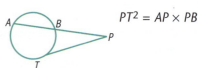

$PT^2 = AP \times PB$

> **Q** Find the value of the pronumeral.
> **A** $PR \times RQ = RT^2$
> $9 \times 4 = 36$
> $\qquad = 6^2$
> $\therefore RT = 6$

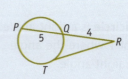

circle, equation of

parts of: The diagrams show the parts of a circle. See the separate entries for their definitions.

properties of: See **chord properties** and **parts of the circle**.

tangent properties:

1 Tangents from an external point are equal.

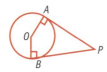   PA = PB

2 The angle between a tangent and a chord is equal to the angle in the alternate segment. See **chord properties**.

3 The tangent is at right angles to the radius at the point of contact.

4 The square of the length of a tangent is equal to the product of the intercepts of a secant drawn from the external point.
See **intersecting chords and secants**, previous page.

circle, equation of The equation of a circle with centre at the origin is: $x^2 + y^2 = r^2$, where r is the radius of the circle.

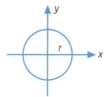

circle graph See **sector graph**. Also called a pie chart.

circumcentre Centre of the **circumcircle**. See this entry.

Excel Junior High School Maths Study Dictionary

circumcircle

circumcircle The circle drawn through the three **vertices** of a triangle. Found by bisecting the sides of the triangle with **perpendicular** bisectors. The circumcircle passes through the three vertices of the triangle. The point of intersection is the **circumcentre**.

Circumference The common name for the boundary of a circle. Given by the formula $C = 2\pi r$, where r is the **radius** of the circle. It could also be thought of as the **perimeter** of a circle. An alternative formula is $C = \pi d$, where d is the diameter.

Q Find the circumference of the circle.
A $C = 2\pi r = 2 \times \pi \times 5 = 10\pi$
  $= 31.4$ cm (to 1 decimal place)

class A group, set or collection of things.

Class	Frequency
1–4	4
5–9	7
10–14	10
15–19	6

centre: The middle score in a class.
For the class 5–9, the class centre is $\frac{5+9}{2} = 7$

size: The largest value less the least value in a class.
For the class 12–16, the class size is $16 - 12 = 4$

class interval The difference between the largest and smallest members of the class. Used with **continuous data**.
For the classes 10 →, 20 →, ... the class interval is 10.

classification

classification Arrangement of items into classes, sets or groups, using characteristics or attributes.

Tall   Middle   Short

classify Sort objects, ideas or events into groups, sets or classes using one or more attributes or characteristics.

clock An analog or digital measuring device for time. One of the most famous clocks was the Harrison Chronometer carried by Captain James Cook on his voyage of discovery to Australia.

closed circle To indicate an inequality on a number line, meaning to indicate that number is included. See also **open circle** and **inequality**.

$-3 \leq x < 4$

Closed curve A curve that returns to its starting point without a break.

simple: A closed curve without an overlap.

complex: A closed curve with at least one overlap.

regular: A circle or an **ellipse**.

 Circle

 Ellipse

C combined shapes

closed shape A closed curve where the sections of the curve are straight lines.

Regular   Irregular

closed operation An operation that produces another element of the set. An operation that achieves closure.
Addition and multiplication of integers are closed.
$3 + 5 = 8$ as 3, 5 and 8 are all integers $3 \times 5 = 15$ as 3, 5 and 15 are all integers.
Note: Division of **integers** is not closed.
For example $3 \div 5$ does not give an integer.

cm The symbol for centimetre. Note: it is not an abbreviation so there is no full stop (.) after cm.

closure See **closed operation**.

cluster A crowding of **data** around a particular score. An example is the rolling of a string of 6s with a die.

co-domain The set of elements from which the dependent variable is selected by the mapping due to the function or relation being considered. See also **domain** and **range**.

coefficient The number or constant multiplying a **variable** in an expression or **equation**.
For $7x^2 - 5x + 3$, 7 is the coefficient of x^2 and -5 is the coefficient of x.
Note: 3 is a constant.

coefficients of polynomials The numbers multiplying the terms of a **polynomial**. For $P(x) = ax^4 + bx^3 + cx^2 + dx + e$, a, b, c, d and e are all coefficients. a is the leading coefficient as it is the coefficient of the term with the highest power.

co-interior angles

Q Give the leading coefficient of
$4x + 3x^2 - 7x^3 + 3x^4$
A The highest power is 4 and the coefficient of the x^4 term is 3. Thus the leading coefficient is 3. Note: The order of terms is unimportant.

co-interior angles The angles contained within a pair of lines and a **transversal**. Also known as allied angles. For **parallel lines** the two angles are supplementary, that is they add to 180°.

$x + y = 180°$

collecting like terms Used to simplify **algebraic expressions**. Like terms have exactly the same combinations of **variables**.

Q Collect like terms for: $7a + 3c - 2a + c^2$.
A The result is $5a + 3c + c^2$.
Note: c and c^2 are not like terms.

collinear Three or more points that lie on a straight line.

column A vertical arrangement.

33
24
7   is a column of figures.

column graph A graph that uses separated columns to represent data. Also called a vertical bar graph. See also **bar graph**. Note 1: There are inconsistent uses of the terms bar and column for graphs.

Note 2: A column graph is used to represent **categorical data** and a **histogram** to represent numerical data.

combination

combination A subset of a set. The ^nC_r button on a calculator generates combinations. See also **Pascal's Triangle**.

> **Q** How many combinations of *A, B* and *C* can be taken two at a time?
> **A** *AB, AC* and *BC* are the three combinations.
> $^3C_2 = 3$ from the calculator.
> Note: Order of selection is unimportant.

combined events In **statistics** and **probability** where two or more simple events occur either together or following each other.
To toss three coins together is a combined event.

combined shapes Shapes that are made from two or more of the standard two dimensional shapes. Also called composite figures. Often used for area questions.

> **Q** Find the area of the combined shape.
> **A** Note: The shape is made up of a trapezium and a square.
> So we find the combined area by finding the two separate areas and adding them.
> $A = 5^2 + \dfrac{8 + 11}{2} \times 4$
> $= 25 + 38$
> $= 63$ cm^2

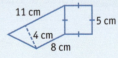

commission An amount paid for a service. Usually associated with sales, calculated as a **percentage** of the sale.
The salesperson earned 1.5% of $800 000 for making the sale of the property. The value of the commission is $800 000 × 0.015 = $12 000.

common denominator For two or more fractions. This is the number that all separate denominators divide exactly. See **denominator** and **lowest common denominator** also.

For $\frac{2}{3} + \frac{3}{5} - \frac{1}{2}$, the common denominator is

$3 \times 5 \times 2 = 30$ as 3, 2 and 5 are all prime.

common difference The property of sequential numbers. The difference between any two consecutive numbers is the same. See also **arithmetic sequence** and **arithmetic series**.
For 1, 4, 7, 10, . . .: $4 - 1 = 7 - 4 = 10 - 7 = 3$ = common difference.

common factor A factor that occurs in more than one term in an expression. Used for factorisation. a is the common factor for $3a + 2ab$ and 3 is the common factor for 6 (3×2) and 9 (3×3).

> **Q1 Factorise $3x^2 + 6x$.**
> **A** The common factor is $3x$, thus
> $3x^2 + 6x = 3x(x + 2)$
> **Q2 Use factors to simplify: $87 \times 6 + 13 \times 6$.**
> **A** $87 \times 6 + 13 \times 6 = 6 \times (87 + 13)$
> $\qquad \qquad \qquad \qquad \; = 6 \times 100$
> $\qquad \qquad \qquad \qquad \; = 600$

common fraction See **fraction**.

common multiple A number that is common to two sets of multiples.
For 2, 4, 6, 8, 10, **12** and 3, 6, 9, **12**, the common multiples are 6 and 12, and 6 is the lowest common multiple of 2 and 3.

commutative property (or law) of addition The order in which an addition is done has no effect on the result. Note: Subtraction is not commutative.
$3 + 4 = 7 = 4 + 3 = 7$. Thus $3 + 4 = 4 + 3$.

C commutative property (or law) of multiplication

commutative property (or law) of multipliction The order in which a multiplication is done has no effect on the result. Note: Division is not commutative.

$3 \times 4 = 12 = 4 \times 3 = 12$. Thus $3 \times 4 = 4 \times 3$.

compare Examine the diagrams or expressions that are given in the question to find similarities and/or differences. To make a comparison.

fractions:

Q1 Compare $\frac{1}{3}$ and $\frac{1}{4}$.

A From the diagrams, $\frac{1}{3} > \frac{1}{4}$.

Q2 Compare $\frac{1}{4}$ and $\frac{2}{8}$.

A From the diagrams $\frac{1}{4} = \frac{2}{8}$.

decimals: See **ascending** and **descending** order of decimals.

compass An instrument that finds the North direction and can thus be used for navigation. The most common forms have a magnetised needle that pivots to point towards **magnetic north**.

compass bearings See **bearings**.

compass rose A figure displaying the orientation of the cardinal directions (N, E, S, W) and the directions in between (NNE, NE, ENE, ESE, SE, SSE, SSW, SW, WSW, WNW, NW, NNW).

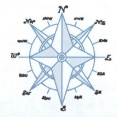

compasses, pair of An instrument used in geometrical constructions together with a straight edge. Used to draw **arcs** and to mark off equal lengths. Often called a compass for short.

complement 1 A quantity that completes a whole. See **complementary addition** and **complementary angles**.
2 The angle that is the difference between a given angle and 90°. See **complementary angles**.

of a set: See **complementary events**, next page.

complementary addition

1 Finding the amount to complete a set.

Q What needs to be added to 12 to give 20?
A 12 + **8** = 20

2 Counting on to a higher total, as in finding change.

Q Find the change from $50 for a sale of $27.
A 27 + 3 = 30, 30 + 20 = 50
The change is $23.

3 As a substitute for subtraction.

Q Subtract 27 from 32.
A 27 + **5** = 32
32 − 27 = 5

complementary angles Two angles that add to a total of 90°.

Q Find the complement of 50°.
A 50 + **40** = 90. The complement of 50° is 40°.

C complementary events

complementary events In **probability**. The probabilities of these two events add to 1. For the event A the complementary event is written A'.
The chance of rolling an even number and the chance of rolling an odd number with a die are complementary events.
Pr(even) = 1 − Pr(odd) and Pr(odd) = 1 − Pr(even).

P(A)   P(A')

completing the square The process to turn a quadratic expression into a **perfect square**. The coefficient of x^2 must be 1.
The x coefficient is halved and then squared. See also **quadratic equation**.

> **Q** Solve by completing the square: $x^2 + 6x + 5 = 0$
> **A** $x^2 + 6x + 5 = 0$ becomes $x^2 + 6x + \left(\frac{6}{2}\right)^2 = -5 + \left(\frac{6}{2}\right)^2$
> and thus $(x + 3)^2 = 4$
> which gives $x + 3 = 2$ or $x + 3 = -2$, $\therefore x = -1$ or $x = -5$.

complex When more than one operation, shape, aspect etc. are performed together or in succession. Used to describe something that is other than simple.

complex fraction A fraction with a fraction as the numerator and/or the denominator.

$\dfrac{\frac{1}{3} + \frac{3}{4}}{\frac{5}{6}}$ is simplified by using the separate operations for the numerator and the denominator.

$$\dfrac{\frac{1}{3} + \frac{3}{4}}{\frac{5}{6}} = \left(\frac{1 \times 4 + 3 \times 3}{12}\right) \div \frac{5}{6}$$

$$= \frac{13}{12} \times \frac{6}{5}$$

$$= \frac{13}{10}$$

$$= 1\frac{3}{10}$$

Excel Junior High School Maths Study Dictionary

complex number Numbers that involve the **square root** of a **negative number**. Used in senior mathematics, especially at university. The basic definition is $\sqrt{-1} = i$.

composite Another word for *more than one*. See **combined shapes**, **composite solids**, **composite numbers**.

composite areas Areas of **combined shapes**. See **Areas**.

composite figures See **combined shapes**.

composite solids, volume of Found by finding the volume of each standard solid and then adding the results.
Find the volume of the figure shown.
The figure consists of a cube and a square pyramid.
Thus the volume is $V = 4^3 + \frac{1}{3} \times 4^2 \times 5$

$= 64 + 26\frac{2}{3}$

$= 90\frac{2}{3}$ cm³

composite numbers A positive **integer** (**natural number**) greater than 1, made up of the product of two other positive integers. There are more than two elements in the factor set. A composite number is not **prime**.
Note: 1 is neither prime nor composite.

> **Q Is 15 prime or composite? Give the factor set.**
> **A** 15 is a composite number as $15 = 5 \times 3$ and $1 \times 15 = 15$.
> The factor set is {1, 3, 5, 15}

compound bar graph See **bar graph, divided**.

compound event An experiment where more than one thing happens.
Example: Selecting two or more marbles from a bag or tossing a coin and a die.

compound interest

compound interest Interest calculations where each interest amount is added to the **principal** before the calculation of the next interest amount. Usually calculated with the formula: $A = P(1 + R)^n$ where $R = \frac{r}{100}$. A is the principal plus interest. n is the number of periods and r is the interest rate per period as a percentage. An alternative form of the formula is $A = P\left(1 + \frac{r}{100}\right)^n$, where r is the rate of interest per period as a percentage.

Q Find the compound interest on $375 at 6% pa for two years, compounded monthly.

A There are 24 periods and the interest rate is $\frac{0.06}{12}$. (6% = 0.06)

Thus $A = 375 \times (1 + 0.005)^{24}$
   $= 422.68$
and the interest is $422.68 - 375 = \$47.68$.

compound operation See **order of operations**.

computation To calculate, work out, find the answer.

compute To calculate, or to find an answer.

Q Compute the simple interest on $1500 at 6% pa for 5 years.

A $I = \dfrac{P \times r \times t}{100}$

$= \dfrac{1500 \times 6 \times 5}{100}$

$= 450$.

The simple interest is $450.

concave A shape that is rounded inwards. The opposite to **convex**.

concave polygon See **re-entrant polygon**.

concentration A rate that is usually calculated as a percentage. It is associated with the purity of dissolved substances. See also **density**.

$$\text{concentration (\%)} = \frac{\text{volume of substance}}{\text{total volume}} \times \frac{100}{1}$$

Example: The concentration of a drink that has 6 mL dissolved in 94 mL of water is $\frac{\text{volume of substance}}{\text{total volume}} \times \frac{100}{1} = \frac{6}{6 + 94} \times \frac{100}{1} = 6$

Thus the concentration is 6%.

concentric circles Circles in the same plane with a common centre.
The region between the circles is the **annulus**.

concurrent lines Three or more lines that pass through a common point. *AB*, *CD* and *EF* all meet at *G*.

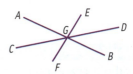

conditional probability

conditional probability The calculation of a chance where a second outcome depends on the first.

> **Q** The diagram shows the number of animals at an animal shelter. What is the probability of selecting a cat given that the animal selected is black?
> B = {black animals} and
> A = {cats}
>
>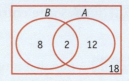
>
> **A** $\Pr(A \mid B) = \frac{2}{10} = 0.2$

Note: $\Pr(A) = \Pr(\text{selecting a cat}) = \frac{14}{40} = 0.35$

$\Pr(A \mid B)$ indicates the probability of event A given that event B has occurred. The sample space is reduced to the set B for the event A.

$\Pr(A \mid B) = \dfrac{\Pr(A \cap B)}{\Pr(B)}$ and $\Pr(A \cap B) = \Pr(A \mid B) \times \Pr(B)$.

cone A solid with a circular base that tapers to a point (**apex**). A circular pyramid.

congruence (≡ or ≅): The property of exact equality. Matching in all respects – shape, size, and area or volume. The property of being identical in shape and dimensions. The usual symbol is ≡.

congruence of polygons When two figures are congruent. See also **congruent triangles**, next page.

congruence transformation A method of changing the position of a shape without changing the shape itself. See **reflection**, **rotation** and **translation**.

congruent triangles

congruent triangles Triangles that have sides equal in pairs and the angles opposite those sides equal in pairs.

tests: There are 4 tests for congruent triangles.

SSS Three sides of one triangle respectively equal to the three sides of the other triangle.

△ABC ≡ △DEF   (SSS)

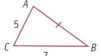

SAS: Two sides of one triangle equal to two corresponding sides of the other and the angle contained by those sides (the included angle) equal.

△ACB ≡ △DFE   (SAS)

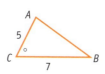 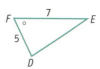

AAS: Two angles and a side are equal to the corresponding angles and side of the other.

△CBA ≡ △FED   (AAS)

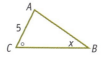

RHS: Two right-angled triangles have equal hypotenuses and a corresponding side equal.

△ACB ≡ △DFE   (RHS)

 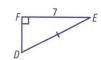

Note: Guard against trying to use the non included angle. This is the ASS case and not a congruency test so you end up being an ass because the triangles are not congruent!

conic section

conic section When a right circular cone is cut by planes at various angles to the axis of the cone, the **ellipse**, **parabola**, **hyperbola**, circle or two straight lines are formed.

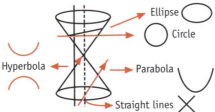

conjecture An unproven theory or idea. A statement whose truth or otherwise is not yet determined. See also **Goldbach's Conjecture**.
There is life elsewhere in the universe.

conjugate surd See **Surd, conjugate**.

connected Two points in the plane are said to be connected if there is a line or curve (edge) that joins them.

connective A logical term that connects or qualifies other expressions. Examples include: *and, or, not, if ... then, is equivalent to*. See also **union** and **intersection**.

consecutive numbers Numbers that follow each other in a sequence with even spacing.
1, 2, 3, 4, 5, . . . $\frac{1}{4}, \frac{2}{4}, \frac{3}{4}, 1, 1\frac{1}{4}, \ldots$
5, 4, 3, 2, 1, 0, –1, –2
They have a **common difference**. See also **arithmetic sequence**.

constant cross-section The characteristic property of prisms where each cross section is the same. See **cross-section**.

constant (term) A number that always has the same value in an **algebraic expression**.
$3x + 6$, 6 is a constant $7y - \pi$, π is a constant.

constraint A condition applied in a particular context.
$x > 0$, n is a **natural number** only, $a \neq 0$ are examples.

construct Make a drawing or drawings. Usually restricted to the use of a pair of **compasses** and a straight edge (ruler).

constructions Done with a pair of **compasses** and a straight edge where equal lengths are found with the compasses as the main basis of the construction. For each construction, the arcs and lines that are the construction lines are shown as feint.

60, 30, 90, 120 degree angles:

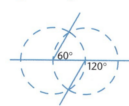

bisecting intervals:

bisecting angles:

circumference of a circle:

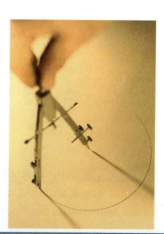

constructions

congruent figures:

parallel lines: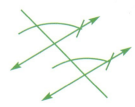

perpendicular lines:

quadrilaterals: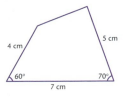

regular polygons on a circle:

triangles: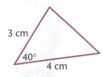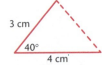

consumables Items that are used in daily activities and requiring constant replacement. Paper and inks, or toner in a printer are examples. Used in consumer arithmetic, next page.

consumer arithmetic

consumer arithmetic The mathematics associated with commercial activities. Includes **commission**, **interest**, **profit**, and **loss** calculations. The application of **percentage** forms a large part of this topic. See the separate entries.

contingency table A rectangular table that shows information for two variables, with one set of categories on the horizontal line and the other set on the vertical line. See **chance, contingency table**.

continue the following An expression that means to produce the next few values in the pattern already started for you.

> **Q** Continue 1, 5, 9, 13, for the next 3 elements:
> **A** 1, 5, 9, 13, **17, 21, 25**

continuous data Data that has no natural gaps, such as height or speed. Can in principle assume all possible values in the interval. In contrast to **discrete data**, it can take any value within an **interval**. An example of numerical data.
An example is the time taken to travel to school.

continuous functions A function without any gaps. As opposed to discontinuity.

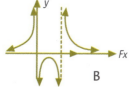

Graph A is continuous while graph B has two discontinuities.

contour lines

contour lines Lines joining points of equal height above sea level on a topological map.

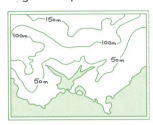 

contracted or abbreviated form Opposite to the **expanded form**.

Q Write $x \times x \times x \times x$ in contracted form.
A $x \times x \times x \times x = x^4$

convergent Moving closer to each other.

converging lines Two or more lines that meet at a point.

AC and BC converge at C

converse An implication that results when the original proposal and the conclusion are interchanged. A converse may or may not be true.
Example: Points lie on a line leads to the converse that lines pass through a point.

conversion graphs Graphs that show a relationship between one quantity and another.
An example is a graph that converts km/h to m/s. They are both examples of a **rate**. See this entry also.

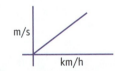

conversions – metric See **convert**, below.

convert Commonly used with measurement (**length**, **area**, **volume**, **capacity**, **time**, etc.). All related to the prefixes: *milli, centi, deci, deca (or deka), hecto* and *kilo*

> **Q Convert 127 m to mm.**
> **A** 127 m = 127 × 1000
>   = 127 000 mm.

convex A shape that is rounded outwards. The opposite of **concave**.

coordinate geometry The part of mathematics that combines **algebra** and plane geometry. Created by Rene Descartes. See **coordinates**, below, and also the entry for **Cartesian coordinates**.

coordinate axes Another name for **coordinates, rectangular**, below.

coordinates

rectangular (cartesian): A pair of numbers that show a unique position in a plane. The first number is the *x* or **independent** value and the second is the *y* or **dependent** value or variable.

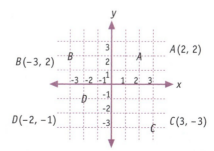

continued over

map reference or seating plan:

 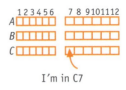

polar: A pair of values that show position in a plane. The first is the distance radially from a fixed point and the second is the amount of turn from a fixed line.

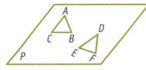

coplanar Lying or being in the same plane.

Triangles *ABC*, *DEF* are in the plane *P*.

copy An instruction that means to write and/or draw what is given in the question on your own paper so that you can use it to complete something (a table or diagram) or use the information given to produce an answer to the question.

correspondence See **one-to-one correspondence**.

corresponding angles

1 Angles in the same or similar position in congruent or similar figures.

corresponding sides

2 Angles formed when two lines are cut by a transversal. See **parallel lines** also.

corresponding sides Sides in the same or similar positions in congruent (equal sides) or similar (sides in the same ratio) figures.

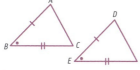

AB corresponds to DE   PQ corresponds to ST $\dfrac{PQ}{QR} = \dfrac{ST}{TU}$

cost price The amount paid for goods or services before selling. See also **selling price**.

cosine ratio Used in trigonometry in a right-angled triangle. It is found by calculating the value $\dfrac{\text{Adjacent}}{\text{Hypotenuse}}$. It is abbreviated as cos. See also **trigonometry**.

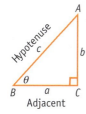

$\cos \theta = \dfrac{BC}{AB} = \dfrac{a}{c}$

A graph can represent the values of the cosine of an angle for angle values from 0° to 360°.

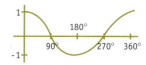

Q Find cos A.
A $\cos A = \dfrac{\text{Adjacent}}{\text{Hypotenuse}}$
$= \dfrac{7}{11}$

C cosine rule

cosine rule   Used in **trigonometry** in non-right angled triangles to find the value of a side or angle.

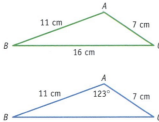

$$\cos A = \frac{b^2 + c^2 - a^2}{2bc},$$
$$a^2 = b^2 + c^2 - 2bc \cos A$$

Q1 Find the value of A.

A $\cos A = \dfrac{b^2 + c^2 - a^2}{2bc}$

$= \dfrac{11^2 + 16^2 - 7^2}{2 \times 11 \times 16}$

$= 0.9318$

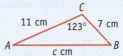

Thus $A = 21° \, 17'$ **Note:** Use [SHIFT] [cos] (Casio) or [2ndF] [cos] (Sharp).

Q2 Find the value of c.

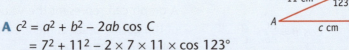

A $c^2 = a^2 + b^2 - 2ab \cos C$
$= 7^2 + 11^2 - 2 \times 7 \times 11 \times \cos 123°$

Thus $c^2 = 253.8744…$ and
$c = \sqrt{253.874}$
$= 15.9$ (to 1 decimal place).

counter example   An instance when a proposition or **conjecture** is false. 6 is a counter-example to the conjecture that every even number is a multiple of 4.

counting The process of listing a subset of the set of counting numbers in consecutive order.

counting numbers The whole numbers commencing with 1.
1 2 3 4 5 6 7 8 9 10, etc.
Note: Zero (0) is not a counting number.

credit cards Plastic cards issued by financial institutions that enable credit to be extended for a purchase. The main providers are American Express, Diners Club, MasterCard, and Visa.

cross method A method of **factorisation** of a **quadratic equation**.

Factorise $3x^2 + 7x - 6$.
$= (3x - 2)(x + 3)$

Must be opposite as no common factor.

cross number puzzle A puzzle based on a square grid when the answers to mathematical operations are written in the space across or down. Similar to a crossword puzzle.

Place the digits in the grid.

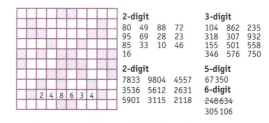

2-digit			3-digit		
80	49	88	72	104	862	235
95	69	28	23	318	307	932
85	33	10	46	155	501	558
16				346	576	750

2-digit			5-digit
7833	9804	4557	67350
3536	5612	2631	**6-digit**
5901	3115	2118	~~248634~~
			305106

cross-section The two-dimensional (2D) shape obtained when a cut is made through a solid at an angle (usually parallel) to the base.

cube 1 To multiply a number by itself twice more. The third power of a number. To multiply a number by the square of that number. See also **cubic number**.
Example: $x^3 = x \times x \times x$
2 A three-dimensional (3D) solid where all 6 faces are equal squares and all angles between the faces are right angles. One of the five **platonic solids**.

cube root The number or value, which when cubed gives the original number. The cube root of 8, written $\sqrt[3]{8}$, is 2 as $2^3 = 8$.

cube, surface area of The surface area of a cube is the sum of the area of the 6 equal faces, all squares.
$SA = 6s^2$, where s is the length of the side.

cubed number See **cubic number**.

cubes, difference of two The subtraction of one cubed value from another. A standard factorisation needed in **algebra**.
$a^3 - b^3 = (a - b)(a^2 + ab + b^2)$

cubes, sum of two The addition of one cubed value to another. A standard factorisation needed in **algebra**.
$a^3 + b^3 = (a + b)(a^2 - ab + b^2)$

cubic centimetre (cm³) A unit of volume measure. It is a cube with sides of 1 cm.
A sugar cube approximately occupies this volume.
A cubic centimetre is written as cm³ and is equivalent to a capacity of 1 mL.

cubic curve The characteristic graph formed from plotting a function with the highest power a cube.
The graph of $y = ax^3 + bx^2 + cx + d$, for $a \neq 0$, has a curve similar to that shown.

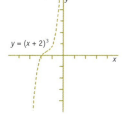
$y = (x + 2)^3$

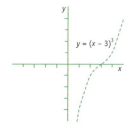
$y = (x - 3)^3$

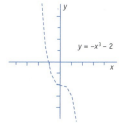
$y = -x^3 - 2$

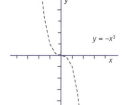
$y = -x^3$

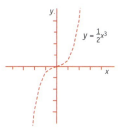
$y = \tfrac{1}{2}x^3$

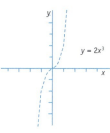
$y = 2x^3$

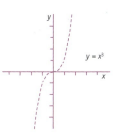
$y = x^3$

cubic decimetre (dm³) A volume equal to a cube of side 10 cm. A litre of water occupies this volume.

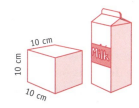

cubic graph See **cubic curve**, above.

cubic metre (m³)

cubic metre (m³) A unit of *volume* measure. It is a cube with sides of 1 m.
A cubic metre is written as m³ and is equivalent to a capacity of 1 kilolitre (kL). $1 \text{ m}^3 = 1\,000\,000 \text{ cm}^3$.

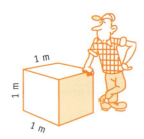

cubic millimetre (mm³) A *volume* equal to a cube of side 1 mm.
$1000 \text{ mm}^3 = 1 \text{ cm}^3$

cubic number A number is cubed when it is multiplied together three times. $2^3 = 2 \times 2 \times 2$ and is read as *2 cubed*, or *2 to the power of 3*. Cubic numbers are 1, 8, 27, 64, 125 . . .

cubic unit A general unit of *volume* measure. It is a cube with sides of 1 unit. Used to indicate a volume when the length measurements given have no specific units.

Q Find the volume of the solid.
A $V = lwh = 4 \times 3 \times 5 = 60 \ u^3$

cuboid An alternative name for a **rectangular prism**. Often two faces are square.

cubit The measurement that Noah used building the ark. It is the length from the tip of the fingers to the elbow. This obviously depends on the size of the person. An example of an informal measure.

cumulative frequency (cf)

cumulative frequency (cf) The progressive summation of the frequencies in a **frequency distribution table**.

Scores	1	2	3	4	5	6	7	8	9	10
Frequency	9	11	6	7	3	5	9	9	4	2
cf	9	20	26	33	36	41	50	59	63	65

cumulative frequency histogram A **histogram** for scores and **cumulative frequency**. The area of each column is proportional to the sum of the frequencies up until and including that score. The next column increases in area (usually by increasing the height) in proportion to the frequency of the next score.

x	f	cf
1	9	9
2	11	20
3	6	26
4	7	33
5	3	36
6	5	41
7	9	50
8	9	59
9	4	63
10	2	65

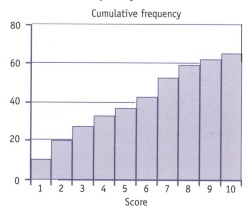

cumulative frequency polygon A plot of the **cumulative frequency** against the upper class boundaries of the scores with the points joined by line segments.

Note: The cumulative frequency histogram is also shown.

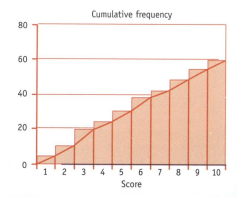

Note: Any continuous cumulative frequency curve is called an **ogive**.

currency, decimal

currency, decimal Money that uses multiples of ten as the basis. For Australia, decimal currency was first introduced on 14th February 1966. 100 cents = $1

curve Usually refers to a line where no part is straight. Technically, straight lines are also curves however. See **curve sketching**.

curve sketching A diagram of a relation or function that shows the intersections and special points such as turning points. In contrast to a graph; which is accurately plotted for all values of the **independent** variable. Curve sketching is intended to be an aid to **algebraic** calculations rather than as a method of solution of the function.

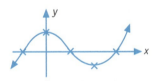

curved surface A surface which is not flat. The surface usually has a regular change of shape. Typical examples include a **sphere** and the sides of **cylinders** and **cones**. See also **plane surface** and **plane shape**.

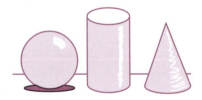

Note: The ends of a cylinder and the base of a cone are not curved.

cyclic quadrilateral

cyclic quadrilateral A **quadrilateral** where all 4 vertices lie on the circumference of a circle.

PQRS is a cyclic quadrilateral.

properties:
1 The opposite angles of a cyclic quadrilateral are supplementary.

$a + b = 180°$
$c + d = 180°$

Q Find the value of *a*.
A $a = 180° - 57° = 123°$.

2 The exterior angle of a cyclic quadrilateral is equal to the opposite interior angle.

Q Find the value of *b*.
A ∡DCE = ∡BAD = b = 135°.

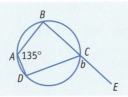

cylinder A **three-dimensional (3D)** solid where the base and cross-section are circular. It is similar to a prism in that the cross section is constant.

continued over

cylinder

volume: Given by the formula $V = \pi r^2 h$, where r is the radius of the base and h is the height of the cylinder.

> **Q** Find the volume of the cylinder.
> **A** $V = \pi r^2 h = \pi \times 5^2 \times 6 = 471.238...$
> ∴ $V = 471.2$ cm³ (to 1 decimal place)

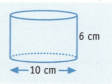

surface area of a closed cylinder: Given by the formula:
$SA = 2\pi r^2 + 2\pi rh$
$\quad = 2\pi r(r + h)$.

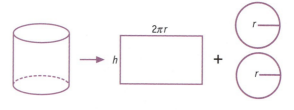

> **Q** Find the surface area of the closed cylinder.
> **A** $SA = 2\pi r(r + h)$
> $\quad = 2 \times \pi \times 5 \times (5 + 6)$
> $\quad = 10 \times \pi \times 11$
> $\quad = 345.575...$
> ∴ the surface area is 345.6 cm² (to 1 decimal place)

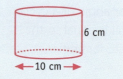

Note: If the cylinder were open at the top:
$SA = 2\pi rh + \pi r^2$
$\quad = 2 \times \pi \times 5 \times 6 + \pi \times 5^2$
$\quad = 60\pi + 25\pi$
$\quad = 267.035...$
∴ the surface area is 267.0 cm² (to 1 decimal place)

data

analysing: The use of **measures of central tendency** (**mean**, **median** and **mode**) and measures of dispersion (**range**, **interquartile range** and **standard deviation**) to describe data and to draw conclusions.

bivariate: Data consisting of two variables that are related and collected together. Examples include height and weight of a group of people or incidence of smoking and state of health. Often plotted as a **scatter diagram**.

collecting: Data are collected in many ways. For data to be useful, the collection requires **random** collection methods that are designed to be unbiased and statistically valid. Data are available through the Australian Bureau of Statistics (ABS) and similar state agencies. See separate entries for **survey**, **observation**, **experiments**, **measurements**, **interview** and **questionnaire**.

grouped: A method of organising data so that results can be found using analysing techniques. A method of enabling **continuous data** to be analysed.

x	0 →	10 →	20 →	30 →	40 → 50
f	5	8	11	7	4

The data are in groups 0 →, 10 → etc

in geometry: Known facts that are accepted without further proof. Used in the process of reaching a conclusion. See also **given**.

over time: Data collected to show changes or trends. Can also be called historical data. Test marks for the year is an example. Often displayed on a line graph or **histogram**.

univariate: Data involving only one **variable**. Such as distance travelled.

daylight saving time (DST)

Standard time during summer when clocks are turned forward one hour to take advantage of evening daylight. NSW, Victoria, Tasmania, Western Australia and South Australia observe DST while Queensland and the Northern Territory do not. See also **time zones**.

D day

day A measure of time. Equal to 24 hours. A measure of one rotation of the Earth on its **axis**.

deca A prefix meaning ten. See also **deka**.

decade A period of ten years. A use of **deca** meaning 10.

decagon A plane figure with 10 sides.

decahedron A solid figure with ten plane faces.

deci A prefix meaning one-tenth. The symbol is d. A decimetre (dm) is one tenth of a metre.

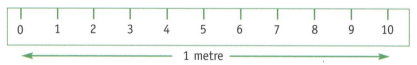

decibel The unit used to measure noise. This is an example of a **logarithmic** scale similar to the **Richter scale** for earthquakes. 10 decibels is barely audible while 140 decibels is the threshold of pain. The noise generated near a rock band's speakers is close to this.

decimal (number)

decimal (number) 1 A number expressed using the base 10 **place value** system.
Example: 416.54 is a decimal number.
2 The common name for a **decimal fraction**.

decimal addition Place the decimal points under each other. Insert zero(s) to fill gaps.

> **Q** Add 4.2 and 3.71
> **A** Use the vertical algorithm   4.2**0**   inserting the 0.
>   + 3.71
>   ──────
>   7.91

decimal division Change the problem to one where the divisor is a whole number.

> **Q** 3.24 ÷ 0.06
> **A** 3.24 ÷ 0.06 becomes 324 ÷ 6 = 54, after multiplying divisor and dividend by 100.

decimal fraction The correct name for numbers less than one that are written using a decimal point.
Example: $0.27 = \frac{2}{10} + \frac{7}{100} = \frac{27}{100}$

decimal multiplication The decimal points are ignored and the multiplication completed. The number of places after the decimal points is then counted and the answer has that many decimal places.
3.25 × 1.7 becomes 325 × 17 = 5525. Three places of decimals are necessary thus the answer is 5.525

decimal places The number of digits to the right of the decimal point.
Example: 8.604 has 3 decimal places.

Excel Junior High School Maths Study Dictionary

D decimal subtraction

decimal subtraction Place the decimal points under each other. Insert zero(s) to fill gaps.

> **Q** Subtract 3.71 from 4.2.
> **A** Use the vertical algorithm 4.2**0**   inserting the 0.
> $$\begin{array}{r} 4.20 \\ -\,3.71 \\ \hline 0.49 \end{array}$$

decimal system The counting system based on the use of the digits 1, 2, 3, 4, 5, 6, 7, 8, 9, 0 and **place value**.

decomposition method of subtraction See **subtraction methods, decomposition**.

decrease Take something off a value, to **subtract**.

> **Q** Decrease 30 by 7.
> **A** This means: 30 − 7 = 23.

Deduction

1 To take away, subtraction.
  Deduct 5 marks for poor setting out!
2 Deductions, **wage**: Amounts taken out of a wage for income tax, Medicare levy, and other items approved by the employee.

deductive geometry Concerned with proofs about general figures. The results are called **theorems** and are proved using basic facts or axioms. **Euclid**, in ancient Greece, recorded much of what we still study today.

deductive reasoning Drawing conclusions from data and/or facts (often geometric) to reach a finding or to prove a result. See also **deductive geometry**, above.

definition D

definition An exact description using only terms that have already been described.

> **Q** Give the definition of an equilateral triangle.
> **A** An equilateral triangle is a plane three-sided figure with all sides equal.

Note: Equilateral is given in terms of equal, plane figure and sides, all terms that have to be defined first.

degree

of an equation: The value of the highest power (**index**) in an equation or expression.
The degree of the equation $x^3 - 5x^2 + 6x - 9 = 0$ is 3.
of a polynomial: The value of the highest power (**index**) in a polynomial.
The degree of the polynomial $P(x) = x^4 - 7x^2 + 5x - 2$ is 4.
as an angle measure: A complete **revolution** is divided into 360 parts called degrees. First used by the Babylonians and so is based on their base 60 numeration system.

as a temperature measurement: Both the **Celsius** and **fahrenheit** temperature scales are measured in degrees. See these entries.

on a calculator:

To enter degrees and minutes: Use the [° ' "] button (*Casio*) or the [D,M,S] button (*Sharp*).

Example: To enter sin 36°25'15": The key strokes are: sin 36 [D,M,S] 25 [D,M,S] 15 [D,M,S] = which gives 0.5937 (to 4 decimal places)

To convert a decimal to degrees and minutes: Use the Shift (*Casio*) or 2ndF (*Sharp*) button with the [° ' "] or [D,M,S] buttons..

Example: Express 36.345° in degrees and minutes. The key strokes are: 36.345 2ndF [D,M,S] = which gives 36°20'42".

deka

deka (deca) Used in the International System of Units (**SI system**) for ten times. Rarely used in Australia. Symbol is da.
A dekametre (dam) is 10 metres and a dekalitre is 10 litres.

delta The fourth letter of the **Greek alphabet**. The symbols are Δ and δ. Used as variables and Δ is also used to represent the **discriminant** in **quadratic equations**.

denominator The bottom numeral in a **fraction**. It shows the size of the fraction. See also **numerator**, the top numeral in a fraction.

$$\text{The fraction } \frac{3}{8} \begin{array}{l} \leftarrow \text{Numerator} \\ \leftarrow \text{Denominator} \end{array}$$

dependent

events: In **probability** where the outcome of a second event depends or is influenced by the first event.
The outcome of drawing a second number from the numbers 1, 2, 3, 4, and 5, depends on the drawing of the first number if the first number is not replaced.

variable: In **co-ordinate geometry** and the number plane.
The y-value given by the equation $y = 3x + 5$ when $x = 2$.
$$y = 3 \times 2 + 5$$
$$= 11$$

density A rate, which is the comparison of **mass** with **volume**. See also **concentration**.

$$D = \frac{M}{V}$$ where D is the density,
M is the mass and
V is the volume.

depreciation A percentage deducted from the book value of an item due to use and age.
A new car depreciates approximately 30% in its first year of ownership.

> **Q** Find the depreciated value after one year of a motor vehicle purchased for $35 000 when the depreciation is 23% pa.
> **A** The value is (100 − 23)% of 35 000 = 77% of 35 000
> $= 35\,000 \times 0.77$
> $= \$26\,950.$

depression, angle of The angle the eye turns through when looking down from the horizontal. It is equal to the **angle of elevation** from the point observed back to the original point.

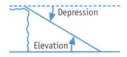

describe
1. Give, in sentence form, a description of something using the properties or other attributes you are expected to identify from the question, or to recall from memory.
2. To mark out or draw.
   Use the pair of compasses to describe an arc.

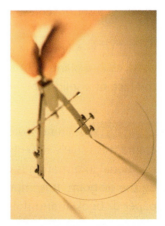

descending order A listing where each number is smaller than the one before.
2.6, $2\frac{1}{2}$, 2.3 2, . . .   Thus $2.6 > 2\frac{1}{2} > 2.3 > 2$
of decimals:

> **Q** Write in descending order:
> 2.1, 2.01, 2.11, 2.001, 2
> **A** 2.11, 2.1, 2.01, 2.001, 2

D descending order

of directed numbers:

Q Write in descending order: 3, −4, +2, 0, −1
A Unsigned values are given + signs.
+3, +2, 0, −1, −4

of fractions:

Q Write in descending order: $2\frac{1}{2}$, 2, $2\frac{1}{4}$, $2\frac{1}{3}$,
A $2\frac{1}{2}$, $2\frac{1}{3}$, $2\frac{1}{4}$, 2

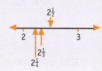

determine
1 An instruction in a question meaning to find or calculate.
Determine the points where the two curves intersect...
2 To specify a figure precisely.
Two points determine a line as only one line can be drawn through any two points. Similarly three points not in a line determine a plane or even a circle in a plane. **Note:** Three points not in a line usually uniquely define a **parabola**.

deviation In **statistics** to show the difference between one number and the **mean** of a set of scores.

diagonal A line joining two non-adjacent **vertices** in a plane figure (**polygon**) or on the face of a solid (**polyhedron**).

Diagonal

diagram A line drawing, graph or picture accompanying a question. The diagram is usually described in full in the text of the question. Sometimes additional information is given in the word part of the question that is not shown on the diagram. It is important to copy the diagram into an examination answers paper or booklet and then mark any additional information on to the diagram.

diameter The chord of a circle that passes through the centre. It is twice the length of the radius. Similarly used with a sphere.

diamond An alternative name for a rhombus. See this entry. Used in baseball and softball.

dice More than one die.

die A regular polyhedron used to determine an outcome. The most common is the cube to give a six-sided die. Another is the regular tetrahedron to give a 4-sided die.
Note: For dice questions always draw a grid showing all possible outcomes before attempting the question.

difference The amount by which one quantity is more or less than another. Found by subtracting the smaller number from the other.

> **Q** Find the difference between 5 and 9.
> **A** The difference between 5 and 9 is the same as the difference between 9 and 5. The result in each case is 4.

difference of two cubes See cubes, difference of two.

D difference of two cubes

difference of two squares When the sum of two terms is multiplied by the difference of the same two terms. Also known as difference of perfect squares (DOPS). See **perfect square**.

$(a + b)(a − b) = a^2 − b^2$

Used in the rationalisation of surds. See entries for **rationalise** and **surd**.

difference of polynomials Collect **like terms** after applying the rule of signs.

Q Find $P(x) − Q(x)$ where $P(x) = 5x^4 + 2x^3 − x + 7$ and $Q(x) = 2x^4 − x^3 + 3x^2 − 1$.
A $P(x) − Q(x) = 5x^4 + 2x^3 − x + 7 − (2x^4 − x^3 + 3x^2 − 1)$
$= 5x^4 + 2x^3 − x + 7 − 2x^4 + x^3 − 3x^2 + 1$
$= 3x^4 + 3x^3 − 3x^2 − x + 8$

digit(s) The numerals 1, 2, 3, 4, 5, 6, 7, 8, 9, 0.

digital Refers to machines and devices that use or display numbers to give a value. In contrast to **analog(ue)** which uses physical quantities to give a value.

Digital

Analog

dihedral angle Refers to the angle between two planes found as the angle between two lines drawn in the planes at right angles to the line of intersection.

dilation

point dilation: the transformation, from a point, of a figure so that it has a similar shape. The new shape may be larger or smaller.
See also **enlargement** and **reduction**.

from an axis: In the example shown dilation by a factor of 2 from the *x*-axis makes a circle transpose to an **ellipse**.

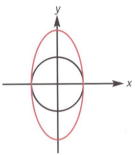

dimensions
The lengths of the sides in a figure.

direct variation (or proportion)
$y = kx$. $y = kx^2$, $v = \sqrt{x}$ etc.
Indicates that the relationship between two variables remains the same ratio as the variables change. Thus they increase together or decrease together. They are said to be related directly. See also **inverse variation (or proportion)** and **partial variation (or proportion)**.
Example: The speed that an object falls is in direct proportion to the height from which it is dropped.

directed number
A number that has a positive or negative sign. +3 is read as *positive 3* or *plus 3,* while −3 is read as *negative 3* or *minus 3*.
Note: *plus* and *minus* are strictly used for addition and subtraction, not for directed numbers.

D directed number operations

directed number operations

addition: Combine the two numbers with signs.

Q1 Find: −2 + 3
A −2 + 3 = +1
Adding a negative number is the same as subtracting a positive number.

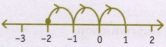

Q2 Find: −3 + −4
A −3 + −4 becomes
−3 − 4 = −7

division: Like signs give a positive. Unlike signs give a negative.

Q1 12 ÷ −4
A 12 ÷ −4 has unlike signs as 12 is +12. Thus
12 ÷ −4 = −3
Q2 −12 ÷ −3
A −12 ÷ −3 has like signs, both negative. Thus
−12 ÷ −3 = +4

multiplication: Like signs give a positive. Unlike signs give a negative.

Q1 12 × −4
A 12 × −4 has unlike signs as 12 is +12. Thus
12 × −4 = −48
Q2 −12 × −3
A −12 × −3 has like signs, both negative. Thus
−12 × −3 = +36 = 36

subtraction: Combine the two signed numbers. The subtraction of a negative becomes an addition of a positive.

Q1 Find −7 − 6
A −7 − 6 = −13
Q2 Find −5 − −4
A −5 − −4 becomes −5 + 4 = −1

discontinuous graph

discontinuous graph A graph where there are gaps or jumps between sections. See also **step graph**.

discount A percentage reduction in the full price. The amount subtracted to give the discounted price. Used in **consumer arithmetic**. See also **mark-down**.

Q Find the discounted price when a discount of 15% is applied to a selling price of $284.
A Discount = 284 × 0.15 = 42.6.
Thus the discounted price = 284 − 42.60 = $241.40.
Note: The discount price is (100 − 15)% = 85% of the original price.

discrete data A quantity having separate and distinct parts. A form of numerical data. Examples include the number of students in a class and the number of days in a month. **Variables** that are not discrete are **continuous data**.

discriminant A value associated with **quadratic equations**. Found using the formula:
$\Delta = b^2 - 4ac$, for the quadratic equation $ax^2 + bx + c = 0$.

D dispersion (measures of)

dispersion (measures of) The spread of the scores from a value, usually the **mean**. The **range**, **interquartile range** and **standard deviation** are examples. See these entries also.
For the values: 3, 5, 7, 7, 9, 11, 14, 16, the range is 16 − 3 = 13.

displacement

1 A change in position, where direction is given as well as distance.
  3 units across followed by 4 units up gives a displacement of 5 in the direction indicated.

2 The amount of liquid that a solid causes to overflow from a filled container. This amount enables the calculation of the volume of irregular shaped objects. This process is also called **Archimedes' principle**.

distance

between two points: $A(x_1, y_1)$ and $B(x_2, y_2)$
Found by using an application of **Pythagoras' theorem**.
$d = \sqrt{(x_2 - x_1)^2 + (y_2 - y_1)^2}$

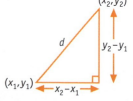

using speed and time: Distance is the product of speed and time, Distance = Speed × Time. This relationship is given by the equation $d = s \times t$, which, in turn gives $t = \frac{d}{s}$ and $s = \frac{d}{t}$.

distributive property

distributive law See **distributive property**, below.

distributive property Enables bracket expansion and **factorisation** using **common factors**. Multiplication is distributed over addition or subtraction. The term outside the brackets multiplies all terms inside the brackets.

$$a(b + c) = a \times b + a \times c = ab + ac \text{ and}$$
$$a(b - c) = a \times b - a \times c = ab - ac$$

divergent To move apart. The arms of an angle are divergent from their point of intersection. The opposite to **convergent**.

divided-bar graph See **bar graph, divided**.

dividend
1 Return on an investment. Payments made by a corporation to its shareholders from past and current earnings. The amount an investor receives is based on the number of **shares** owned.
2 The value being divided.

$$\text{divisor} \overline{\smash{)}\text{dividend}}^{\text{quotient}} + \text{remainder}$$

dividing a quantity in a ratio The process to separate the quantity into parts that match the given **ratio**; by first dividing by the total of the number of parts and then multiplying by the particular ratio.

> **Q** Divide $15 in the ratio of 3:2.
> **A** $3 + 2 = 5$, thus $15 \div 5 = 3$. ∴ The two parts are $3 \times 3 = \$9$ and $3 \times 2 = \$6$

D dividing polynomials

dividing polynomials Use the long division algorithm. Divide by the leading term and match appropriate terms.

Q $(2x^3 + 5x^2 - x - 6) \div (x + 2)$

A
$$
\begin{array}{r}
2x^2 + x - 3 \\
x+2\overline{\smash{)}2x^3 + 5x^2 - x - 6} \\
\underline{2x^3 + 4x^2} \\
x^2 - x \\
\underline{x^2 + 2x} \\
-3x - 6 \\
\underline{-3x - 6} \\
0
\end{array}
$$

divisible When a number can be divided exactly by another number.
12 is divisible by 12, 6, 4, 3, 2 and 1

divisibility tests Methods to see if a number can be divided by another without actual division. These tests are useful in **factorisation**.

2: A number is even.
  Example: 16 is divisible by 2 as 16 is even.
  $(16 = 2 \times 8)$
3: The sum of the digits is divisible by 3.
  Example: 522 is divisible by 3 as
  $(5 + 2 + 2) \div 3 = 9 \div 3 = 3$ $(522 = 3 \times 174)$
4: The last two digits are divisible by 4.
  Example: 2044 is divisible by 4 as $44 \div 4 = 11$. $(2044 = 4 \times 511)$
5: Ends in a 0 or 5.
  Example: 20 and 4025 are both divisible by 5.
  $(20 = 5 \times 4$ and $4025 = 5 \times 805)$
6: The number is divisible by both 2 and 3.
  Example: 432 is divisible by 6 as it is even and
  $(4 + 3 + 2) \div 3 = 9 \div 3 = 3$. $(432 = 6 \times 72)$
7: There is no simple test.
8: The last 3 digits are divisible by 8.

division D

Example: 5656 is divisible by 8 as 656 ÷ 8 = 82. (5656 = 8 × 707)
9: The sum of the digits is divisible by 9.
Example: 2115 is divisible by 9 as (2 + 1 + 1 + 5) ÷ 9 = 9 ÷ 9 = 1. (2115 = 9 × 235)
10: Ends in 0.
Example: 20, 200 and 2000 are all divisible by 10. (2000 = 10 × 200)
11: The sums of the odd placed digits and even placed digits are the same or differ by a multiple of 11.
Example: 6204 is divisible by 11 as 6 + 0 = 2 + 4. (6204 = 11 × 564) and 180 708 ÷ 11 = 16 428 (8 + 7 + 8 − 1 = 22)

division The process of partitioning the set into subsets of equal size.
of algebraic functions: See **cancelling**.
of decimals: Change the problem to one where the divisor is a whole number.

> **Q** 3.24 ÷ 0.06
> **A** 3.24 ÷ 0.06 becomes 324 ÷ 6 = 54, after multiplying **divisor** and **dividend** by 100.

See also **division of whole numbers**, next page.
of directed numbers: Use the rule of signs.
Like signs give + and unlike signs give −.

> **Q** Find **i** −6 ÷ (−3) **ii** 14 ÷ (−2) **iii** −8 ÷ 2 **iv** +12 ÷ (+3)
> **A i** Like signs give +. Thus −6 ÷ (−3) = +2
> **ii** Unlike signs give −. Thus 14 ÷ (−2) = −7.
> **iii** Unlike signs give −. Thus −8 ÷ 2 = −4.
> **iv** Like signs give +. Thus +12 ÷ (+3) = +4.

of fractions: Multiply by the **reciprocal** (inverse) of the dividing fraction.

> **Q** $\frac{3}{4} \div \frac{5}{8}$
> **A** $\frac{3}{4} \div \frac{5}{8} = \frac{3}{4} \times \frac{8}{5} = \frac{6}{5} = 1\frac{1}{5}$

continued over . . .

D divisor

of polynomials: See **dividing polynomials**. Also see **long division**.

of surds: The division of a surd by a surd is the same as the surd of the division.

Q $\dfrac{\sqrt{21}}{\sqrt{7}}$

A $\dfrac{\sqrt{21}}{\sqrt{7}} = \sqrt{\dfrac{21}{7}}$
$= \sqrt{3}$

of whole numbers:

Single digit division uses **short division**.

Q Find $324 \div 5$

A $6\ 4$
$5\overline{)32^24}\ r\ 4$

Multiple digit division uses **long division**.

Q Find $2317 \div 16$

A
$$\begin{array}{r} 144 \\ 16{\overline{\smash{\big)}\,2317}} \\ \underline{16} \\ 71 \\ \underline{64} \\ 77 \\ \underline{64} \\ 13 \end{array}$$

divisor   The value that is dividing another. See **dividend**.

dodeca   A **prefix** that means twelve.

dodecagon   A twelve sided polygon.

Excel Junior High School Maths Study Dictionary

dodecahedron A twelve-faced **polyhedron**. One of the five **platonic solids**.

domain The set from which the **independent variable** is chosen in a **function** or relation. See also **co-domain** and **range**.

dops Difference of perfect squares. See **difference of two squares**.

dot

diagrams: Used in **statistics** to display outcomes. Similar to an **array**.

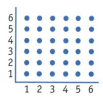

plot: A vertical arrangement of data on a number line where each dot represents a unit. Also called a **dot plot** or an **ordinate diagram**.

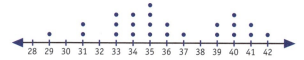

dotted line A line that is not solid. A line with breaks in it. Used to show hidden sides in a solid and for lines not included in regions with linear inequalities. Also called a **broken line**. See also **linear inequations**.

double Twice as much, to multiply by 2.
The length of AB is double the length BC.

double-time An hourly rate of payment for work done when that work is done outside normal working hours. See **penalty rates**.

dozen A group of 12. Most commonly used in packaging of items such as eggs and soft drinks.

duodecimal A system of counting by twelves. The last example we have is the use of dozen. Also old units of length (12 inches to the **foot**) and money (12 pence to the shilling) that disappeared with the introduction of decimal measurement in Australia in 1966.

e
Euler's number (approximately equal to 2.718). Used as the basis of **natural** or **Naperian logarithms**.

earnings
Salary or wages paid for services rendered or goods exchanged.

edge(s), of three-dimensional (3D) shapes
The line where two faces meet. Also the straight line or curve that forms the **boundary** of a region in the plane.

EFTPOS
(Electronic Funds Transfer Point Of Sale): The method by which a machine and a plastic card are used to make a transfer of funds to affect a sale of goods or services.

Egyptian numerals
Used by the ancient Egyptians. An additive system with a new symbol for each power of 10.

element
A member of a set. An undefined term. 5 is a member of the set $S = \{1, 3, 5, 7, 9\}$. This can also be written as $5 \in S$.

elevation, angle of
When looking upwards, the angle of elevation is the angle between the line of sight and the horizontal. Equal to the angle of depression of the original point from the elevated point. See also **depression, angle of**.

E elimination method

elimination method For the solution of **simultaneous equations**. The **coefficients** of one of the variables are made equal by multiplication. One equation is then subtracted from the other, eliminating one of the variables (unknowns).

Q Solve simultaneously
$2x + 3y = 8$
$3x - y = 1$

A $2x + 3y = 8$ become $6x + 9y = 24$ ($\times 3$)
$3x - y = 1$ becomes $6x - 2y = 2$ ($\times 2$)
This gives $11y = 22$ after subtraction.
The result $y = 2$ follows.
Substituting $y = 2$ into the second equation gives $3x - y = 1$
The result $x = 1$ follows.

ellipse A regular closed curve. Also called an **oval**. The path of a point moving so that the sum of its distances from two fixed points remains the same.

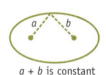

$a + b$ is constant

embedded Inserted as part of a whole. Usually refers to one solid forming part of a larger complex solid.

The cube is embedded in the solid shown.

empirical Refers to data or evidence collected by observation, measurement or experiment. As opposed to evidence produced by **deductive reasoning**.

empty Refers to a set with no elements. It is also called the null set. Represented by either ϕ or $\{\ \}$.

enantiomorphic A mirror image relationship between two **asymmetric** objects. An example is a pair of gloves or your hands.

enlargement   E

enlargement The increasing in size of an object by multiplying by a scale factor. See **dilation** and **reduction**. The angle relationships remain the same. One of the transformations (**reflection**, **rotation**, **translation** and **dilation**). The scale factor is greater than 1.
This is an enlargement of the original photograph.

enlargement factor Scale factor, see **enlargement** above and **dilation**.

entire A shape with all sides that flex outwards away from the centre. See also **convex** and **concave**.

entire surd A surd where the only numeral is the number under the square root sign.

Q Express $3\sqrt{2}$ as an entire surd.
A Express $3\sqrt{2} = \sqrt{3^2} \times \sqrt{2} = \sqrt{18}$

envelope A curve that is a tangent to every member of a family of curves. See also **cardioid**.

equal additions method of subtraction See **subtraction methods**, **equal additions**.

Excel Junior High School Maths Study Dictionary

E equal

equal The same value or amount. Uses the symbol (=).

equally likely See **chance (probability), equally likely**.

equality The state of being **equal**.

equation A relationship between variables that contains an equal sign (=). See also **expression, algebraic**.
Note: The difference between an equation and an expression is the existence of an equals sign in the equation.
$y = 2x + 3$, $x^2 + 7x + 6 = 0$ and $3x + 2 = 3(2x - 1)$ are examples of equations.
one-step: An equation which needs only one step to find the solution.
$x + 6 = 9$ is a one-step equation as it requires only the subtraction of 6 from both sides to give the result $x = 3$
solving – linear equations: Involves isolating variables on one side of the equation from numbers on the other side.
$x + 2 = 3(2x - 1)$ becomes
$x - x + 2 + 3 = 6x - x - 3 + 3$ and $5 = 5x$. Thus $x = 1$
solving – quadratics: Factorise and then equate factors to zero.
$x^2 + 7x + 6 = 0$ becomes $(x + 6)(x + 1) = 0$, giving
$x + 6 = 0 \Rightarrow x = -6$ and $x + 1 = 0 \Rightarrow x = -1$.
solving – polynomials: Factorise as for quadratics and then equate factors to zero.
$2x^3 + 5x^2 - x - 6 = 0$ gives $(2x + 3)(x + 2)(x - 1) = 0$, then $2x + 3 = 0$ or $x + 2 = 0$ or $x - 1 = 0$. Thus $x = \frac{-3}{2}$, $x = -2$ or $x = 1$.
two-step: An equation where two processes are needed to get the answer.
$3x - 4 = 8$ is a two-step equation as it requires **i** the addition of 4 to both sides and **ii** the division of both sides by 3.
$3x - 4 + 4 = 8 + 4$ giving $3x = 12$ and then $3x \div 3 = 12 \div 3$ which gives $x = 4$.

equation of straight line

The intercept form is $y = mx + c$ or, $y = mx + b$ where **m** is the gradient of the line and **b** or **c** is the y-intercept.
The general form is $ax + by + c = 0$, where a, b and c are all constants and **a** is positive.

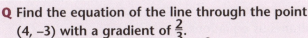

To obtain the equation given:
point and gradient: use the formula
$y - y_1 = m(x - x_1)$ where
m is the gradient and (x_1, y_1) is a point on the line.

> **Q** Find the equation of the line through the point (4, −3) with a gradient of $\frac{2}{3}$.
> **A** $y - y_1 = m(x - x_1)$ gives $y - -3 = \frac{2}{3}(x - 4)$. This then gives $3y + 9 = 2x - 8$ and finally $2x - 3y - 17 = 0$.

two points: use the formula: $\frac{y_2 - y_1}{x_2 - x_1} = \frac{y - y_1}{x - x_1}$,
where (x_1, y_1) and (x_2, y_2) are the points.
Note: You could also use the point gradient form after first using the two points to find the gradient.

> **Q** Find the equation of the line through the points A(3, −2) and B(−5, 3)
> **A** $\frac{y_2 - y_1}{x_2 - x_1} = \frac{y - y_1}{x - x_1}$ gives $\frac{-2 - 3}{3 - -5} = \frac{y - 3}{x - -5}$, and $\frac{-5}{8} = \frac{y - 3}{x + 5}$.
> This then gives $-5x - 25 = 8y - 24$ and finally $5x + 8y + 1 = 0$.

equations

equivalent: A description of the series of equations formed when a linear equation is solved for the unknown.
$3x + 6 = 15$ becomes $3x = 9$ and this becomes $x = 3$. The 3 equations are equivalent as they all represent the value of $x = 3$.

exponential: See **exponential equations**.

continued over

E equator

equations, literal: An alternative name for a **formula**. $A = \pi r^2$, is the formula for the area of a circle.

of straight lines: Written in either the **intercept form** $y = mx + b$ or the **general form** $ax + by + c = 0$.

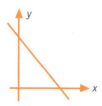

quadratic: See **quadratic equation**.
simultaneous: See **simultaneous equations**.

equator A circle that divides a sphere into two equal and symmetric halves. A place on the Earth's surface that has latitude of 0°.

equiangular All angles in the figure are equal. A rectangle is equiangular as all angles are right angles.

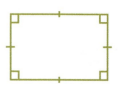

equiangular triangle A triangle with all three angles equal. See **equilateral triangle**, next page.

equidistant The same distance from two or more objects or points.
For example the centre of the circle is equidistant from every point on the circumference.

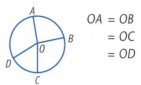

equilateral All sides in the figure are equal.
The hexagon has all sides equal.

equilateral triangle A triangle with all three sides equal. When the sides are equal the angles are equal and thus an **equiangular** triangle as well.

equilibrium A position of rest or balance.

equivalent 1 In **algebra**: Equal in value or amount. See also **expression, algebraic**.
   $3(2x - 5) + 5(x - 3)$ is **equivalent** to $11x - 30$ after simplification.
   The symbol $\Leftrightarrow$ is used to show equivalence.
2 In **geometry**: The same as each other though expressed in different form.
   The angles *ABC* and *ABD* are equivalent.

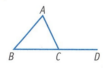

equivalent fractions Fractions that are a multiple of another fraction.
$\frac{12}{16} = \frac{2 \times 6}{2 \times 8} = \frac{6}{8} = \frac{2 \times 3}{2 \times 4} = \frac{3}{4}$, thus $\frac{12}{16}$, $\frac{6}{8}$ and $\frac{3}{4}$ are all equivalent fractions.
ratios: Where one ratio is a multiple of the other.
200:300 is equivalent to 2:3.

E   Eratosthenes, sieve of

Eratosthenes, sieve of Named after the Greek mathematican and astronomer Eratosthenes, 276-195 BC. A method of finding prime numbers by elimination of multiples of primes. Called a sieve because it is believed that the numbers were punched out when eliminated on the original parchment. Various arrangements of numbers are used. When numbers are grouped in columns of 6, straight lines identify all prime numbers.

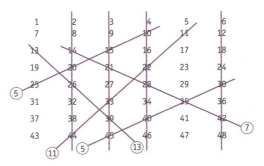

Note: Multiples of 2 and 3 cancel vertically |||
Then multiples of 5 diagonally /
Then multiples of 7 diagonally \
Then multiples of 11 diagonally /
Then multiples of 13 diagonally \. etc.

error The difference between the true value of an amount and a measurement of it. The theoretical value of an error in measurement is half of the least measure. The value is always positive:
error = |measurement − actual value|.
If a measurement is taken to the nearest metre then the error is ± 0.5m.

Escher, Maurits A Dutch graphic artist, 1898-1972, who created many line prints with mathematical themes. Tessellation formed the basis of many of these. See also **tessellation**.

escribed circle A circle that has one side of a triangle and the other two sides extended as tangents.

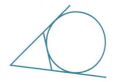

estimate Use the information given and/or your experience to give an approximate answer without working out an exact value. This is often done by rounding the numbers involved to the nearest 10 or 100 etc. Can also be used to indicate the estimation of quantities such as length, mass and area.
What is the estimate of the mass of this book?

estimation The rounding off of numbers to obtain an approximation to the exact answer in a calculation.
An estimate for 17×147 *is* $20 \times 150 = 3000$.

> **Q** Give an estimate of 37×442.
> **A** The multiplication becomes $40 \times 440 = 17\,600$.

Euclid (Euclidean) A Greek mathematician, c300 BC, who wrote *Elements,* the detailed record of Greek mathematics that still forms the basis of the (Euclidean) geometry studied in schools today. See **geometry**.

Euler's theorem (formula) Named after Swiss mathematician Leonard Euler, 1707-1783, founder of modern mathematical analysis. Gives a relationship between the **faces** (*F*), **edges** (*E*) and **vertices** (*V*) of all polyhedra, including that for a prism or pyramid. See **polyhedron**.
Faces plus vertices equals edges plus 2. $F + V = E + 2$

Evaluate An instruction that means *to calculate* or *to find the value of.* Carry out one or more operations to get the result and then clearly present the result below the calculations. Similar to **calculate**.

E even (natural)

even (number) A number that is divisible by 2. See also **odd numbers**. 2, 4, 6, 8, 10, . . . are the even numbers.

event In **statistics**, an experiment or an **observation** or the **outcome** of an experiment.
in probability: A subset of the possible outcomes of an experiment (sample space).
Example: For {1, 2, 3, 4, 5, 6}, $E = \{2, 4, 6\}$ where E is the event, even numbers in the sample space.

exa A prefix meaning a million million million. (10^{18}). Its symbol is E.

exact Means accurate or correct in every way. Not approximate. Used with **surds** and in **trigonometry**. To give the answer as it comes from the calculation, without rounding. Often includes special values like π or an **irrational number**.
The exact ratio for $\sin 60° = \frac{\sqrt{3}}{2}$

Q Find the exact area of a circle of radius 6 cm.
A The formula $A = \pi r^2$ gives $A = \pi \times 6^2 = 36\pi$. The exact area is 36π cm^2.

examine Have a good look at something and then attempt to make a conclusion.

Q Examine the following and state which step is incorrect.
$3x + 2 = 8$
$\quad 3x = 10$
$\quad\quad x = \frac{10}{3}$
$\quad\quad\quad = 3\frac{1}{3}$
A The second line is incorrect, as the correct step is $3x + 2 - 2 = 8 - 2$, which gives $3x = 6$ and thus $x = 2$.

expand

example An instance where a proposition or conjecture is true.

expand An instruction to write out in full; often associated with **brackets**. To remove the brackets.

> **Q** Expand and collect terms:
>   i $3(x + 2)$
> **A** $3(x + 2) = 3 \times x + 3 \times 2$
> $= 3x + 6$
>   ii $x(3x + 2)$
> **A** $x(3x + 2) = x \times 3x + x \times 2$
> $= 3x^2 + 2x$
>   iii $5x(7 + 2x)$
> **A** $5x(7 + 2x) = 5x \times 7 + 5x \times 2x$
> $= 35x + 10x^2$, or $10x^2 + 35x$.
>   iv $(x + 2)(x - 3)$
> **A** $(x + 2)(x - 3) = x(x - 3) + 2(x - 3)$
> $= x \times x - x \times 3 + 2 \times x - 2 \times 3$, which gives $x^2 - 3x + 2x - 6$
> $= x^2 - x - 6$

expand and simplify An instruction, usually in **algebra**. Remove the brackets and collect like terms.

> **Q** $3(x - 2) - 5(3 - 2x)$
> **A** $3 \times x - 3 \times 2 - 5 \times 3 - 5 \times -2x$
> $= 3x - 6 - 15 + 10x$
> $= 13x - 21$.

expanded form Involves the use of powers of 10 to express a number. Also called expanded notation. See also **index notation**.

decimals:

> **Q** Show 0.124 in expanded form.
> **A** $0.124 = 1 \times \frac{1}{10} + 2 \times \frac{1}{100} + 4 \times \frac{1}{1000}$ as fractions of 10.
> $= 1 \times 10^{-1} + 2 \times 10^{-2} + 4 \times 10^{-3}$ as powers of 10.

continued over

expanded form in algebra

whole numbers:

Q Write 12 459 in expanded form.
A $12\,459 = 1 \times 10\,000 + 2 \times 1000 + 4 \times 100 + 5 \times 10 + 9 \times 1$
as multiples of 10.
$= 1 \times 10^4 + 2 \times 10^3 + 4 \times 10^2 + 5 \times 10^1 + 9 \times 10^0$

expanded form in algebra Write the expression with operation signs $(+, -, \times, \div)$.

Q Write $3x^2$ in expanded form.
A $3x^2 = 3 \times x^2$
$= 3 \times x \times x.$

expansion A longer form, equivalent to the original or given form. Often means to remove brackets.

Q Give $(x - 1)^3$ in expanded form.
A $(x - 1)^3 = (x - 1)(x - 1)(x - 1)$
$= x^3 - 3x^2 + 3x - 1.$

expected value The number of times that event is expected to occur from a certain number of trials. $E(x) = n \times p$, where n is the number of trials and p is the probability of success of the event. The expected value is theoretical only.

Q If a fair coin is tossed 500 times, how many heads are expected?
A p = probability of a head = $\frac{1}{2}$. Thus $E(head) = n \times p = 500 \times \frac{1}{2} = 250$.

Note: We can expect 250 heads in theory. The actual result may not be exactly that amount on any 500 tosses.

expenses Payments made by a business or an individual. Used in creating a budget. These can be fixed (payments of loans, mortgages and other regular charges) and variable (clothing, food and entertainment). See also **budget**.

experiment A controlled **observation** of an activity with consideration of outside influences and a careful recording of all outcomes. A form of data collection.

experimental probability The calculation of the **relative frequency** of an event occurring.
Relative frequency = $\frac{\text{frequency of score}}{\text{total frequency}} = \frac{f}{\Sigma f}$.
Note: Σ means sum of.

Q For the data:

x	1	2	3	4	5
f	4	7	11	5	3

find the relative frequency of a score of 2.

A relative frequency = $\frac{f}{\Sigma f} = \frac{7}{30}$. Thus the experimental probability of a 2 is $\frac{7}{30}$.

exponent Alternative name to **index** or **power**. In $3^4 = 81$, 4 is the exponent.

exponential Description of the use of an index. See **index** and **exponential equations**, and also **exponential graphs**, next page.

exponential decay When there is a decrease in the value for an increase in the variable. The graph slopes down to the right. The equation is of the form $y = a^{-x}$.

E exponential equations

exponential equations Equations involving exponents (indices) as the unknown.
$2^x = 64$ is an example; which is solved by using powers. $2^x = 64 = 2^6 \therefore x = 6$

exponential graphs ($y = a^x$) A graph where the **independent variable** is an exponent (**index**). The principal characteristics are that the range is always greater than zero and when the independent variable equals zero, the **dependent variable** is 1.

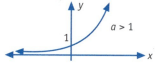

exponential growth When there is an increase, at an increasing rate, in the value for an increase in the variable. The graph slopes up to the right. The equation is of the form $y = a^x$.

exponential notation See **index form**.

exponential relationship See **exponential equations** above.

expression, algebraic Numbers and **pronumerals** separated by operation signs (+, −, ×, ÷). A collection of terms.
Note: The difference between an expression and an equation is that there is an equals sign in the equation.
$x^2 + 6x - 3x^2 + 2 - x + 8$ is an expression while
$x^2 + 6x - 3x^2 + 2 - x + 8 = 0$ is an equation.

extend An instruction; to continue. Usually used in **geometry**.
Extend the line AB to C.

114 Excel Junior High School Maths Study Dictionary

exterior angle

exterior angle

of a triangle: The angle formed when one side of a triangle is extended.

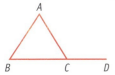 $\hat{ACD}$ is an exterior angle. 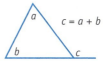 $c = a + b$

Note: The exterior angle of a triangle is equal to the sum of the two opposite **interior angles**.

of a polygon: The angle formed when one side of a polygon is extended.

 $\hat{FAG} = \hat{BCH}$ are exterior angles.

sum of: The sum of the exterior angles of all convex polygons is 360°.

 $a + b + c + d + e + f + g + h = 360°$.

extract An instruction; to find the value of.

Q Extract the square root of 2.
A This means; find the square root of 2, ie $\sqrt{2}$.

extrapolate To estimate a value by following a pattern or graph and then going beyond the values already known (either larger or smaller). The values obtained are only an estimate based on the values known. See also **interpolate**. Used in **graphs** and **statistics**.

F f

f The most used symbol for function. Note: *g(x)* and *h(x)* are other function notations. *The function $f(x) = 3x^3 - 7x + 5$.*

face A bounded surface or a bounded region in a **network**.

faces of 3D shapes The flat surfaces of a solid.

factor A factor of a whole number divides it exactly. *1, 2, 3, 4, 6 and 12 are all factors of 12.*

factored form When the **common factor** is taken outside the brackets of the other forms.

> **Q** Put $3x^2 - 9xy$ in factored form.
> **A** $3x^2 - 9xy = 3x(x - 3y)$

factors Two or more whole numbers that multiply together to give another number. Prime factors are factors that are **prime numbers**.

> **Q** Factorise 42 into its prime factors.
> **A** $42 = 7 \times 6$
> $ = 7 \times 3 \times 2.$

factor theorem for polynomials $(x - a)$ divides $P(x)$ if and only if $P(a) = 0$. The theorem is used to find factors by substitution into the polynomial.

> **Q** Is $(x - 3)$ a factor of $P(x) = x^4 - 5x^3 + x^2 + 7x + 4$?
> **A** $P(3) = 3^4 - 5 \times 3^3 + 3^2 + 7 \times 3 + 4$
> $ = 81 - 135 + 9 + 21 + 4$
> $ = -20 \neq 0$
> Thus $(x - 3)$ is not a factor.

factor tree A diagrammatic representation of the complete **factorisation** of a number into its **primes, factors**.

$$\therefore 24 = 3 \times 2 \times 2 \times 2$$
$$= 3 \times 2^3$$

factorial The continued multiplication of positive integers from 1 to the number indicated. $5! = 5 \times 4 \times 3 \times 2 \times 1 = 120$ and generally $n! = n(n-1)(n-2)(n-3) \times \ldots \times 3 \times 2 \times 1$

factorisation Used in **algebra**. The reverse of expansion; that is find common factors and thus insert brackets. See also **expansion**.
The factorisation of $3x + 6y = 3(x + 2y)$ through the use of the common factor 3. There are several factorisation techniques.
by change of variable: When an equation has higher powers or terms in brackets raised to powers, a substitution is made to simplify the equation and thus enable a factorisation.
To solve $x^4 - 7x^2 + 6 = 0$, first substitute $x^2 = X$
to give $X^2 - 7X + 6 = 0 \Leftrightarrow (X-6)(X-1) = 0$
which leads to the final result, $(x + \sqrt{6})(x - \sqrt{6})(x+1)(x-1) = 0$ $x = \pm\sqrt{6}$ or $x = \pm 1$.
Similarly $(x+2)^2 + 3(x+2) + 2$ is factorised by first substituting $(x+2) = a$, giving $a^2 + 3a + 2 = (a+2)(a+1)$. Thus the final factorisation is found by substituting back: $(x+2+2)(x+2+1) = (x+4)(x+3)$.
by common factor:

> **Q** Factorise:
> i $3x + 6$
> **A** The common factor is 3: $3x + 6 = 3 \times x + 3 \times 2$
> $\qquad\qquad\qquad\qquad = 3(x + 2)$
>
> ii $3x^2 + 2x$
> **A** The common factor is x
> $3x^2 + 2x = x \times 3x + x \times 2$
> $\qquad\quad = x(3x + 2).$
> iii $10x^2 + 35x$
> **A** The common factor is **5x**:
> $10x^2 + 35x = 5x \times 2x + 5x \times 7$
> $\qquad\qquad\quad = 5x(2x + 7).$

continued over

factorisation

by grouping in pairs: This process produces an intermediate stage of taking out **common factors** in two groups and this leads to the final factorisation.

Q Factorise: A: $5x^2 - 10x - 3ax + 6a$.
A Group in pairs:
$5x^2 - 10x - 3ax + 6a = 5x(x - 2) - 3a(x - 2)$
$= (x - 2)(5x - 3a)$.

difference of two squares: Based on $a^2 - b^2 = (a + b)(a - b)$.

Q Factorise: $x^4 - y^4$.
A $x^4 - y^4 = (x^2 - y^2)(x^2 + y^2) = (x + y)(x - y)(x^2 + y^2)$

difference of two cubes: Based on $a^3 - b^3 = (a - b)(a^2 + ab + b^2)$.

Q Factorise $27x^6 - y^3$.
A $27x^6 - y^3 = (3x^2)^3 - y^3$
$= (3x^2 - y)[(3x^2)^2 + 3x^2 \times y + y^2]$
$= (3x^2 - y)(9x^4 + 3x^2y + y^2)$

sum of two cubes: Based on $a^3 + b^3 = (a + b)(a^2 - ab + b^2)$.

Q Factorise $27x^6 + 64y^9$.
A $27x^6 + 64y^9 = (3x^2)^3 + (4y^3)^3$
$= (3x^2 + 4y^3)[(3x^2)^2 - 3x^2 \times 4y^3 + (4y^3)^2]$
$= (3x^2 + 4y^3)(9x^4 - 12x^2y^3 + 16y^6)$

quadratic trinomials: See **quadratic equations**.

fair An experiment where all the outcomes are equally likely. See also **fair game**, below.

fair game A game where the chance of success is equal to the chance of failure so there is no advantage to one player or the other. An example of a fair game is two-up when heads and tails are the only acceptable outcomes.
See also **unfair game**.

f-angles Alternative name for **corresponding angles**. See this entry.

farthest The longest distance away.

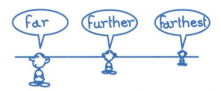

fathom An imperial measurement of depth equal to 6 feet or 1.8288 m, associated with ships and the sea. A depth in water; especially related to navigable water. Originally derived from the length of a man's outstretched arms.

fees A payment for a service at a rate set by the provider of the service; such as a doctor, lawyer, engineer or agent.

fibonacci numbers Named after the Florentine mathematician Leonardo Fibonacci, 1180-1250. A sequence of numbers that describes natural phenomena. After the first two each new number is the sum of the previous two.
1, 1, 2, 3, 5, 8, 13, 21, 34, 55, 89, 144, . . .
(1 + 1 = 2), (1 + 2 = 3), (2 + 3 = 5), etc
The sum of a group of Fibonacci numbers is 1 less than the number, two places, further on. For example: 1 + 1 + 2 + 3 + 5 + 8 + 13 = 34 − 1 = 33.

F figurate numbers

figurate numbers Sequences of whole numbers named after geometrical figures such as triangles, squares and pentagons.

Square numbers   Triangular numbers   Pentagonal numbers

figure A name for a solid, shape, line or numeral.

find An instruction. See **evaluate**.

financial year A period of one year over which income accounts must be calculated for an individual. The financial year is from July 1 to June 30 in Australia.

finite A quantity that is countable or a figure that has a boundary or limit. See also **infinite**.
{a, b, c, d} is an example of a finite set.

first The one at the beginning.
In the sequence: 5, 9, 13, 17, . .   the first number is 5.

fixed expenses Payments of loans, mortgages, rent, rates and other regular charges. See also **budget** and **variable expenses**.

flat Being in one plane only.

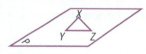

Triangle XYZ is in the plane P for two dimensions.   ABC is one plane, ACD is another for three dimensions.

Excel Junior High School Maths Study Dictionary

flat rate (of interest) Used in association with finance and especially with **loan** calculations. An alternative name for simple interest. The interest is calculated on the original value of the loan right up to the point when the loan is paid off in full. See **simple interest** and also **reducible rate of interest**.

flexible A jointed structure is flexible when its angles can be changed by moving the struts without altering their size or arrangement. See also **rigid**, which is the opposite.

a rectangle is flexible

a triangle is not flexible

flexiday A day able to be taken off work and the time deficit from hours required to be worked to be made up later or prior to the day off.

flexitime A set number of hours are to be worked within a defined time. The start and finish and time for breaks such as lunch are able to be varied.

flip To turn over to give the reflected image. Usually left to right. *When we flip the symbol ⌞ we get ⌟. This is a left to right **reflection**.*

flowchart A diagram that shows a sequence of steps to achieve a result. Widely used in computer programming and in production schedules.

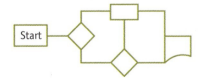

formal unit A unit whose value is fixed by agreement. **Litre** is a formal unit of capacity for fluids and **hour** is a formal unit of time.

formula(e) Used in **algebra** and many calculations. An equation used to find a value. Formulae is the plural. The formula for the area of a circle is: $A = \pi r^2$.

F foot

foot 1 The bottom of something. The foot of the flagpole; the foot of the **perpendicular**.

2 An imperial measure of length. Approximately 30 cm.
1 foot = 12 inches.

fortnight Literally fourteen nights. Two weeks or 14 days.

fractal Any pattern that reveals greater complexity as it is enlarged.

fraction (notation) A **rational number** of the form $\frac{a}{b}$, where a and b are **integers** and $b \neq 0$.
$\frac{a}{b} = \frac{\text{numerator}}{\text{denominator}}$. Also called a simple fraction, common fraction or vulgar fraction.

fraction

addition: First express each separate fraction with the same (lowest common) **denominator** (bottom numeral) and then add the resultant **numerators** (top numerals).

Q Find $\frac{2}{3} + \frac{3}{5}$.

A $\frac{2}{3} + \frac{3}{5} = \frac{2 \times 5 + 3 \times 3}{15}$
$= \frac{10 + 9}{15}$
$= \frac{19}{15}$
$= 1\frac{4}{15}$, after simplifying.

fraction

fraction, algebraic: Obey the same rules as numeric fractions.

addition and subtraction: A common denominator is found for addition and subtraction.

Q1 Find $\dfrac{3a}{4} - \dfrac{2a}{3}$.

A $\dfrac{3a}{4} - \dfrac{2a}{3} = \dfrac{3a \times 3 - 2a \times 4}{12} = \dfrac{9a - 8a}{12} = \dfrac{a}{12}$.

Q2 Find $\dfrac{5}{a-1} - \dfrac{2}{a+1}$.

A $\dfrac{5}{a-1} - \dfrac{2}{a+1} = \dfrac{5(a+1) - 2(a-1)}{(a-1)(a+1)}$

$= \dfrac{5a + 5 - 2a + 2}{(a-1)(a+1)}$

$= \dfrac{3a + 7}{(a-1)(a+1)}$

division: Takes advantage of cancelling after inversion of the divisor and multiplying before finally multiplying numerators and denominators separately.

Q Find $\dfrac{abc}{d} \div \dfrac{ac}{d^2}$.

A $\dfrac{abc}{d} \div \dfrac{ac}{d^2} = \dfrac{abc}{d} \times \dfrac{d^2}{ac}$

$= bd$

multiplication: Takes advantage of cancelling before multiplying numerators and denominators separately.

Q Find $\dfrac{12a^2}{5x} \times \dfrac{x^2 y}{4a}$.

A $\dfrac{12a^2}{5x} \times \dfrac{x^2 y}{4a} = \dfrac{3axy}{5}$

fraction, division: Multiply by the inverse of the dividing fraction. Division is achieved through multiplication by the **inverse**.

Q $\dfrac{3}{4} \div \dfrac{5}{8}$.

A $\dfrac{3}{4} \div \dfrac{5}{8} = \dfrac{3}{4} \times \dfrac{8}{5}$

$= \dfrac{6}{5}$

$= 1\dfrac{1}{5}$

F fractions in equations

fraction, multiplication: Multiply the numerators to produce the new numerator and the denominators to produce the new denominator. See also **cancelling** and **mixed numerals**.

Q Find $\frac{5}{9} \times \frac{3}{8}$

A $\frac{5}{9} \times \frac{3}{8} = \frac{5 \times 3}{9 \times 8}$

$= \frac{5}{24}.$

fraction, subtraction: First express each separate fraction with the same (lowest common) denominator and then subtract the resultant numerators.

Q Find $\frac{3}{4} - \frac{2}{3}$

A $\frac{3}{4} - \frac{2}{3} = \frac{3 \times 3 - 4 \times 2}{12}$

$= \frac{9 - 8}{12}$

$= \frac{1}{12}.$

fractions in equations The fraction is first removed by multiplying each term by the common denominator. The equation is then solved in the normal manner.

Q1 Solve for x: $\frac{2x + 5}{3} - \frac{x - 1}{4} = 7.$

A $\frac{2x - 5}{3} - \frac{x - 1}{4} = 7$ becomes $\frac{12(2x + 5)}{3} - \frac{12(x - 1)}{4} = 12 \times 7$ and thus $4(2x + 5) - 3(x - 1) = 84$

This then solves: $8x + 20 - 3x + 3 = 84$ then

$5x + 23 = 84$ and $5x = 61$ or $x = 12\frac{1}{5}.$

Q2 Solve: $\frac{3}{x} + \frac{5}{x^2} = 2.$

A $\frac{3}{x} + \frac{5}{x^2} = 2$ becomes $\frac{3x^2}{x} + \frac{5x^2}{x^2} = 2x^2$ and then $3x + 5 = 2x^2.$

Thus $2x^2 - 3x - 5 = 0 = (2x - 5)(x + 1).$

Thus $x = \frac{5}{2}$ or $x = -1$

$= 2\frac{1}{2}.$

fraction bar The common name for the line between the numerator and denominator in a fraction. Its correct name is the **vinculum**.

fraction conversion
decimals: Divide the numerator by the denominator after inserting a decimal point.

Q Express $\frac{3}{8}$ as a decimal.

A Complete the division. $8\overline{)3.000}$ giving 0.375. Thus $\frac{3}{8} = 0.375$.

to percentage: Multiply the fraction by 100.

Q Express $\frac{3}{8}$ as a percentage.
A $\frac{3}{8} = \frac{3}{8} \times \frac{100}{1}\% = \frac{300}{8}\%$ or 37.5%.

Note: The equivalent decimal can also be multiplied by 100 to give the result.

fractional Index See **index notation, fractional index**.

freezing point The temperature at which ice melts. This is 0°C. This value together with the boiling point of water, 100°C, defines the **Celsius** temperature scale.

frequency Used in **statistics**. The number of times a score occurs.

frequency distribution (table) A graph or table showing how often an event occurs.

x	1–10	11–20	21–30	31–40	41–50
f	5	8	11	7	4

The values of f are called grouped frequency, see **data, grouped**.

F frequency diagram

frequency diagram A frequency graph. See separate entries for **box-and-whiskers diagram**, **cumulative frequency histogram**, **cumulative frequency polygon**, **frequency histogram**, **frequency polygon** (both below) and **stem-and-leaf plot (table)**.

frequency histogram A column graph with no gaps between the columns. The score is plotted on the horizontal axis and the frequency on the vertical axis. The area of each column is proportional to the frequency of that score.

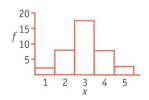

frequency polygon A specialised line graph. The score is plotted on the horizontal axis and the frequency on the vertical axis. The area under the polygon is proportional to the frequency of that score.

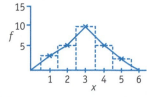

Note: The polygon is plotted on the midpoints of the columns of the histogram. Note also the endpoints on the horizontal axis.

front view A diagram of an object, as seen from directly in front. Also called the front elevation when referring to plans of an object or building. See also **top view** and **side view**.

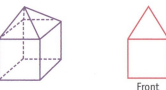

Front

frustum A **pyramid** or **cone** cut by a plane parallel to the pyramid's base.

fully factored form This form of the expression has the highest common factor outside the brackets.

Q Express $3(a^2 - ab)$ in fully factored form.
A $3(a^2 - ab) = 3a(a - b)$.

fuel consumption A rate. A measure of the performance of a motor vehicle. Usually measured in litres per 100 km (L/100 km).

function 1 A rule that assigns to every input value a unique output value.

Q For $f(x) = x^3 - 7x^2 + 5x - 3$ find $f(-2)$.
A $f(-2) = (-2)^3 - 7 \times (-2)^2 + 5 \times (-2) - 3$
$= -8 - 28 - 10 - 3$
$= -49$

2 A correspondence (map or relation) between the elements of two sets. Either one-to-one or many-to-one.
inverse: See **inverse function**.
notation: $f(x) = x^3 - 7x + 5$, $g(x) = 9 - 4x$ are two examples.
Thus $f(3) = 3^3 - 7 \times 3 + 5 = 11$ and $g(-1) = 9 - 4(-1) = 13$.
vertical line test: If a vertical line can be drawn to cut a graph in at most one place only then the graph represents a function.

Thus a function

Thus not a function

furlong An **imperial measurement** (a furrow long). One eighth of a mile. Lately used in measurement of horse race distances. Approximately 201 m.

G g

g 1 The symbol for the mass unit, gram. See **gram**.
2 The symbol for gravity. See **gravity**.

gain An increase, or a move in the positive direction. The opposite of **loss**.
The temperature moved from −4°C to +2°C, a gain of 6 degrees.

gallon An **imperial measurement** for capacity. One gallon is equal to approximately 4.55 L.

gear ratio Ratio of the number of teeth on one sprocket compared to those interlocked on another sprocket. Also includes sprockets joined by a chain.

 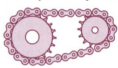

general form of the equation of a line Used in **coordinate geometry**.
$ax + by + c = 0$, where a, b and c are constants and $a \geq 0$.

> **Q** Give $y = 7x + 3$ in general form.
> **A** Rewrite the equation: $y - y = 7x + 3 - y$ to give $7x - y + 3 = 0$.

general form of the quadratic equation Used in **algebra**.
$ax^2 + bx + c = 0$, where a, b and c are constants and $a \neq 0$.

general term Non-specific term, often described using a **formula** that uses the position of the term.
Example: The nth term of an arithmetic sequence is $T_n = a + (n-1)d$

generate An instruction: To find an answer, usually for a series of numbers.

> **Q** Generate the next 4 numbers in the sequence: 1, 4, 7, ...
> **A** The sequence is increasing by +3 each term. Thus 1, 4, 7, 10, 13, 16, 19.

geodesic The shortest path drawn on a curved surface, joining two points. On a *sphere* this is a *great circle*.

geometry The part of mathematics that studies the relationships, properties and measurements of points, lines, angles, planes and solids. The major study at school is based on Euclid's *Elements*, the detailed record of Greek mathematics that still forms the basis of the (**Euclidean**) geometry studied in junior high school.
Note: There are other geometries — co-ordinate geometry and non-Euclidean geometries being two groupings.

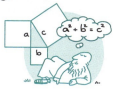

geometric constructions See *constructions*.

geometric progression See *progression*.

geometric series See *series*.

giga (Symbol G) A prefix meaning one thousand million. A gigalitre (1GL) = 1 000 000 000 L = 1×10^9 L.

give An instruction that means: Carry out any calculations and then write down your answer.

given Something that is known. Also called **data**. Used in formal statements such as the proof of congruence or similarity of triangles.

give reasons An instruction that means: Back up the value you have calculated by the theory that allows you to find the value. Most frequently the reason will be the statement of a **theorem** in geometry.

GMT Greenwich Mean Time. The time at the **prime meridian** which passes through the observatory at Greenwich, in greater London, UK. Also known as UTC: Universal Time Coordinate. See **longitude**.

Goldbach's conjecture Named after Prussian mathematician Christian Goldbach, 1690-1764. Every even number ≥ 4 is equal to the sum of two **prime numbers**. First postulated by Goldbach in 1742 to **Euler**.

$4 = 2 + 2 \quad 6 = 3 + 3 \quad 8 = 3 + 5$
$10 = 3 + 7 \quad 12 = 5 + 7 \quad 24 = 11 + 13$

golden ratio (phi φ) See **golden rectangle**, below.

golden rectangle (mean or section) For a rectangle, the sides are in the approximate ratio of 1:0.618. The relationship was first identified by the ancient Greeks. It is considered pleasing to the eye and is widely used in art and the built environment.

Note: The exact value is given by $1 : \dfrac{2}{1 + \sqrt{5}}$.

googol One of the largest named numbers. Reportedly named by a child for his mathematician father. It is 1 followed by 100 zeros. 1×10^{100}.
Note: The Internet search engine Google was named after this number, but became 'Google' because of a spelling mistake on a cheque from investors when it was founded.

googolplex Considered to be the largest named number. It is a googol raised to the power of a googol. $(1 \times 10^{100})(1 \times 10^{100})$.

gradient (m) The slope of a line, found by dividing rise (increase in height) by run (distance travelled horizontally). See also **coordinates** and **equations**.

gradient formula For the line joining the points $A(x_1, y_1)$ and $B(x_2, y_2)$.

$m = \dfrac{y_2 - y_1}{x_2 - x_1} = \tan \theta$, where θ is the angle the line makes with the positive direction of the x-axis, $x_1 \neq x_2$.

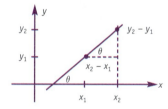

gradient-intercept form of the equation of a line
Used in **coordinate geometry**.
$y = mx + b$ or $y = mx + c$. m is the gradient and b or c is the y-intercept.

> **Q** Give the gradient and y-intercept for the line represented by the equation $3x - 2y + 5 = 0$.
>
> **A** Rewrite the equation in the gradient intercept form.
> $3x - 2y + 2y + 5 = 0 + 2y$ becomes $2y = 3x + 5$ and $y = \frac{3}{2}x + \frac{5}{2}$.
> Thus the gradient is $\frac{3}{2}$ and the y-intercept is $\frac{5}{2}$.

G gradient-intercept method of sketching

gradient-intercept method of sketching To sketch a straight line by plotting the y-intercept and then using the gradient value to obtain another point. Note: The gradient and intercept can be used to find the equation. See **gradient-intercept form** on the previous page.

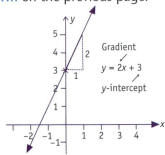

graduated Marked with a measurement scale.

Ruler in centimetres

Thermometer in degrees

gram A metric unit of mass.
Its symbol is g.
1000 g = 1 kg

graph An instruction that means: Draw an accurate graph with pencil and ruler, usually on grid paper. A sketch is not sufficient.
Graph the function $f(x) = x^2 - 5x + 6$.

x	−4	−3	−2	−1	0	1	2	3	4
y	42	30	20	12	6	2	0	0	2

graphs See separate listings for:
bar graph (chart), bar graph, divided
conversion, cumulative frequency histogram
cumulative frequency polygon
dot plot
exponential graphs ($y = a^x$)
frequency histogram, frequency polygon
line graphs, logarithmic, graphs
parabola
scatter diagram, sector graph (pie)
step graph, stem-and-leaf plot (table)
travel graphs

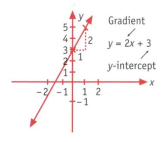

graph paper See grid paper.

graphics Computing term used to describe pictures, photos and drawings.

graphics calculator Also known as a **graphing** or graphical calculator, is a type of a hand-held calculator that can be used to plot graphs, solve equations and performing many other tasks with variables. They are often programmable and have large displays for graphing. Used for graph-based maths such as **trigonometry** and **statistics**.

graphing
on the number line: Place a dot on the point. A group of points is connected with a line. If an end point is not included in the set, the dot is open.

$-1 < x \le 2$

continued over

G graphs of patterns

graphing, on the number plane: Pairs of values are plotted as points. The points have the format (x, y) where the x value is the distance on the horizontal or independent axis (**abscissa**). The y value is the distance on the vertical or dependent axis (**ordinate**). These points are also called **ordered pairs**. Also called the Cartesian plane. See also **Cartesian coordinates**.

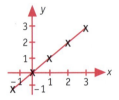

The join of these points gives the graph of the relationship.

graphs of patterns   See graphing on the number plane. The plotting of ordered pairs that represent a pattern produced by a pattern rule in **algebra**.

gravity   The force of attraction exerted by one object on another. Most commonly applied to the force on an object close to the surface of the Earth. The force appears as the weight of the object. Represented by the symbol g and has an approximate value of 9.8 m/s^2.

great circle   The shortest distance between two points on a sphere. The equator and the meridians of longitude are examples of great circles. See also **geodesic** and **small circle**.

greater than (>)   A relationship where the value to the left is larger than the value to the right of the symbol.
Examples: −4 > −7   4 > 1

greatest common divisor (gcd) See **HCF (highest common factor)**.

greater than or equal to (≥) A relationship where the value to the left is larger than, or equal to, the value to the right of the symbol.
Examples: −4 ≥ −7   −4 ≥ −4   8 ≥ 6

greek letters Angles are sometimes assigned letters from the Greek alphabet. Common letters are θ (theta), α (alpha), β (beta), γ (gamma) and φ (phi).

Greenwich meridian See **longitude**.

grid A network of parallel lines, similar to grid paper.

grid diagram A use of a grid to express outcomes in **probability**. See **array**.

grid paper Paper marked with lines arranged in a regular pattern. Also called graph paper. Used for graphing or drawing.

grid references An ordered pair giving rectangular co-ordinates on a map. Usually given as a letter and a number (B, 5). See also **graphing, on the number plane**, previous page.

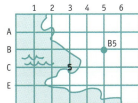

gross

gross An older measurement grouping associated with **imperial measurements**. Equal to 144; a dozen dozen. See also **duodecimal**.

gross, to Means total. For example gross weight or gross income.

gross mass The total mass of an object and its container. The mass of the container is called the tare.

Tare weight   3.2 t
Gross   8.6 t

gross pay or income The pay an employee is credited with before any deductions are made. See also **net pay** or **income**.

group A specific collection of things. 23 = 2 groups of 10 and 3 units.

grouped data See **data, grouped**.

grouped frequency See **data, grouped**.

grouping symbols **braces** { }, **brackets** [ ] and **parentheses** ( ) are the most common examples – all usually called brackets. The **square root** symbol $\sqrt{3 \times 5}$, and the **vinculum** (fraction bar) $\frac{3 \times 5}{2 + 3}$ are other examples. Mainly used to override the **order of operations**. See the individual entries.

guess, check and refine (trial and error) A method of solving **equations** by making an estimate of the result, then substituting that value to enable a second, more refined, estimate and so on.

H

h Symbol for **height**. See this entry.

Symbol for **hour**. See this entry.

Symbol for **hecto**. See this entry, next page.

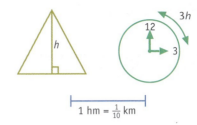

ha Symbol for **hectare**. See this entry, next page.

half One of two equal parts. Represented by the fraction $\frac{1}{2}$ and the decimal 0.5.

half plane The region defined by a **linear inequation**. See this entry.

halve, to An instruction: To divide into two equal parts.

hand The measurement unit for the height of horses, which is measured from the ground to the top of the front leg shoulder. Approximately the width of an adult's palm.

handspan An informal unit of measure. The distance between the tip of the thumb and the tip of the smallest finger.

H HCF (highest common factor)

Hanoi, Tower of See **Tower of Hanoi**.

HCF (highest common factor) The largest factor of two or more numbers. See also **factor trees**.

> **Q** Find the HCF of 15 and 24.
> **A** As $15 = 5 \times 3$ and $24 = 8 \times 3$, the HCF is 3.

hectare A **metric** measure of area. It has a value of $10\,000$ m^2.

hecto The prefix that means 100 times.

height The measurement of the distance from the top to the bottom (or base) of an object or figure.

helix The curve that comes from drawing a straight line on a plane sheet and then wrapping that around a cylinder or cone.

A screw thread is an example.

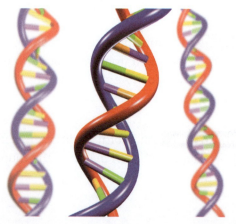

The DNA molecule is a double helix.

hemisphere Half of a **sphere**. The cut is along a great circle.

heptagon A seven-sided plane figure.

hexadecimal A number system based on 16. Used especially with computers. Symbols: 0, 1, 2, 3, 4, 5, 6, 7, 8, 9, A, B, C, D, E, F

hexagon A six-sided plane figure.

hexagram The shape formed by two intersecting equilateral triangles. A regular hexagram is the Star of David, which is on the flag of Israel.

hexagonal

numbers: Numbers that form hexagonal patterns. 1, 6, 15, 28, 45, . . .

H hexahedron

hexagonal prism: A prism with a hexagonal base.

hexagonal pyramid: A pyramid with a hexagonal base.

hexahedron A solid with six faces. All cuboids are hexahedrons. The cube is a regular hexahedron. One of the five platonic solids.

hexomino A plane figure made from six equal squares which meet at least one full side to one full side each. The basis of the strategy game Hexominos.

hieroglyphics See Egyptian numerals.

highest common factor See HCF.

Hindu-Arabic numerals The numerals used almost universally in the world today. Invented by Hindus (from India) around 300BC and carried to Europe by the Arabs who invaded Spain in the eighth century. The symbols have changed over time. The current symbols are 1, 2, 3, 4, 5, 6, 7, 8, 9, 0. Used with the base ten numeral system.

hire-purchase A name given to the process of having possession of goods while paying for them, with interest, over a period of time by regular payments. Now more correctly called a lease agreement.

histogram A version of the **column graph** used in statistics. There is no separation between the columns. See also **cumulative frequency histogram**.

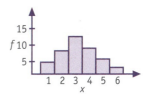

holiday loading Under Australian working conditions all employees are eligible for a 17.5% additional payment for four weeks of their base pay. Originally intended to replace **penalty rate** payments while the employee is on leave. Introduced in Australia in the early 1970s.

home loan See **loan**.

horizon The line at which the earth's surface and sky appear to meet.

H horizontal axis

horizontal axis In a graph or on the **number plane**, the left-right axis. See also **vertical axis**.

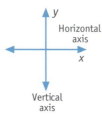

horizontal line A line parallel or level to the horizon. See also **vertical line**. Slope of **zero**.

horizontal surface Any surface that is parallel or level with the horizon. To be level.

hour A measure of time. One twenty-fourth of the time the Earth takes to make one rotation on its axis.
1 hour = 60 minutes   24 hours = 1 day

hourly rate of pay The amount paid to a wage earner for one hour of work. It is the basis on which wages are usually calculated. See also **double time** and **time-and-a-half**.

hundreds column The third column in the **algorithm** for addition or subtraction of **whole numbers**.

```
  hundreds
    tens
     ones
  2  3  6
+    6  7
─────────
  3  0  3
```

hundredth The amount obtained when a quantity is divided into 100 equal parts. Represented by the fraction $\frac{1}{100}$ or the second place after the decimal point (0.01).

hyperbola A group of curves that are constrained between fixed lines called **asymptotes**.
rectangular: A curve asymptotic to a pair of lines at right angles. Typical equations include $y = \frac{1}{x}$, $y = \frac{a}{x}$ and $y - k = \frac{a}{x - h}$, where **a**, **h** and **k** are constants and **x** and **y** are variables and $a \neq 0$.

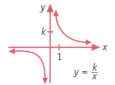
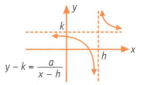

non-rectangular: A curve asymptotic to a pair of lines that meet at any angle other than a right angle. See also **asymptotes**.

hypotenuse The name of the longest side in a **right-angled** triangle. The side opposite the right angle. The origins of the word relate to the suspension of a right angle under a diameter in a circle.

hypothesis A statement that appears to explain some observations, but which has not yet been tested. See also **null hypothesis**.

i The symbol used to represent the number $\sqrt{-1}$. This class of numbers is called the complex numbers. An older name is **imaginary numbers**, see below.

icosahedron A solid with 20 faces. The regular icosahedron is one of the five **platonic solids**. Each face is an **equilateral triangle**.

identical Exactly alike.

identity (element) A value that when combined with another element under **addition** or **multiplication** leaves the other element unchanged.
0 is the identity element for addition. $\qquad a + 0 = a$
1 is the identity element for multiplication. $\qquad a \times 1 = a$

image An exact copy of an object.

imaginary numbers The original name for the set of **complex numbers**. This set is based around the concept of being able to set a value to $\sqrt{-1}$ as ***i***.

Imperial measurements Measurements using the **yard**, the **pound** and the **gallon** as the standard units of length, mass and capacity. Originally used in the United Kingdom (UK) and then throughout areas colonised by the English. Now used mainly in the UK and the USA. The system is characterised by a great variety of conversion factors.

implication A statement of the form *if … then*. An implication is true unless the first part of the statement is true but the second part is false.

impossible event The event that can not occur. Has **zero** likelihood (chance) of occurring. A logical or mathematical impossibility.

> **Q** Give the probability that the sun will set in the east.
> **A** The probability that the sun will set in the east is 0, as it is an impossible event.

improper fraction A fraction where the numerator is greater than the denominator. See also **mixed number**.
$\frac{15}{7}$ is an improper fraction. It is equal to $2\frac{1}{7}$, as a mixed number.
To convert improper fractions to mixed numbers and the mixed numbers back to an improper fraction with a calculator:

> **Q1** Convert $\frac{8}{3}$ to a mixed number.
> **A** Enter 8 $a^b/_c$ 3 = to give 2 ⌐ 2 ⌐ 3 (*Casio*) or
> 8 $a^b/_c$ 3 = to give 2r2r3 (*Sharp*).
> $\frac{8}{3} = 2\frac{2}{3}$
>
> **Q2** Convert $2\frac{2}{3}$ to an improper fraction.
> **A** Enter 2 $a^b/_c$ 2 $a^b/_c$ 3 = SHIFT $a^b/_c$ to give 8 ⌐ 3 (*Casio*) or
> 2 $a^b/_c$ 2 $a^b/_c$ 3 = SHIFT $a^b/_c$ to give 8r3 (*Sharp*).
> $2\frac{2}{3} = \frac{8}{3}$

incentre The centre of the circle drawn inside a triangle which touches each side of the triangle. See **incircle**, next page.

inch An imperial length measure. Approximately 2.54 cm. See also **foot** (=12 inches).

incircle

incircle A circle drawn inside a triangle so that it touches each side of the triangle.

> **Q** Construct the incircle for the given triangle.
> **A** Bisect each of the angles of the triangle. The point of intersection is the incentre. Place the pair of compasses on this point and open to touch one side. Then draw the incircle.

inclination The angle between two lines; between a line and a plane; or between two planes. See also **elevation, angle of** and **depression, angle of**.

included angle The angle between two sides of a triangle. When two sides and the included angle are given the triangle can be constructed.

income Money earned for a service provided. **Wages, salary, commission** and service charges are examples.

increase An instruction: To make larger by the addition of a certain amount or by multiplying by a given number.

> **Q1** Increase $3 by 25 cents.
> **A** 3.00 + 0.25 = 3.25. The increased value is $3.25.
>
> **Q2** Increase the amount of $2000 by 250%.
> **A** 2000 × 2.5 = 5000. Thus the increased amount is $2000 + $5000 = $7000

increasing To grow greater.

independent events Events where the outcome of one event does not influence the other event. Associated with the domain of the relation. See also **chance, (probability)** and **dependent, events**.
Example: *The tossing of a coin does not influence the roll of a die.*
Two events A and B are independent if $Pr(A) = Pr(A|B)$ or $Pr(B) = Pr(B|A)$. Independent events can also be written as $Pr(A \cap B) = Pr(A).Pr(B)$.

independent variable The variable that when substituted for into an equation or a function gives the value of the **dependent variable**.
In $f(x) = x^3 - 7x + 3$ and $y = 5x^2 - 3x + 2$, ***x*** is the independent variable.

index form To write a continued product as an index. See also **exponential notation**. $a \times a \times a \times a = a^4$ and $a \times a \times a \times ... \times a$ (for *n* terms) $= a^n$

index laws **first index law:** multiplication $a^m \times a^n = a^{m+n}$
second index law: division $\quad a^m \div a^n = a^{m-n}$
third index law: zero index $\quad a^0 = 1, (a \neq 0)$
fourth index law: power to power $\quad (a^n)^m = a^{n \times m}$
fifth index law: index of product $\quad (a \times b)^n = a^n \times b^n$

continued over

index notation

sixth index law: index of quotient $\left(\dfrac{a}{b}\right)^n = \dfrac{a^n}{b^n}$, $b \neq 0$

seventh index law: negative index $a^{-n} = \dfrac{1}{a^n}$

Note: $\left(\dfrac{a}{b}\right)^{-n} = \left(\dfrac{b}{a}\right)^n$, $a \neq 0$ and $b \neq 0$.

eighth index law: fractional index $a^{\frac{1}{n}} = \sqrt[n]{a}$

Note: $\sqrt[n]{a}$ is called the surd form.
See also **index operations**, below.

index notation

The indication of repeated multiplication. For $2^4 = 16$, 2 is called the base, 4 the index and 16 the basic numeral.
$a \times a \times a \times a \times a = a^5$

fractional index: Indicates a root.
$a^{\frac{1}{3}} = \sqrt[3]{a}$ and $a^{\frac{2}{3}} = (\sqrt[3]{a})^2$

negative index: Indicates a fraction.
$a^{-3} = \dfrac{1}{a^3}$ and $a^{-\frac{3}{5}} = \dfrac{1}{a^{\frac{3}{5}}} = \dfrac{1}{\sqrt[5]{a^3}}$ or $\dfrac{1}{(\sqrt[5]{a})^3}$ where both results are the same, only the order of the root and power are reversed.

zero index: Any quantity to a zero index is equal to 1.
$a^0 = 1$ and also $(a^3 \times a^4)^0 = 1$
See also **index laws**, above.

index operations

addition: Only exactly the same terms with the same powers can be added.
$a^3 + a^3 = 2a^3$, while $a^2 + a^3$ has no result other than $a^2 + a^3$ or $a^2(1 + a)$.

subtraction: Only exactly the same terms with the same powers can be subtracted.
$4a^3 - a^3 = 3a^3$, while $3a^2 - a^3$ has no result other than $3a^2 - a^3$ or $a^2(3 - a)$.

multiplication: For the same variable, the indices are added.
$a^3 \times a^5 = a^{3+5} = a^8$ and $4a^6 \times 3a^4 = 4 \times 3a^{6+4} = 12a^{10}$

division: For the same variable, the second index is subtracted from the first.
$a^3 \div a^5 = a^{3-5} = a^{-2} = \dfrac{1}{a^2}$ and $4a^6 \div 3a^4 = 4 \div 3 \times a^{6-4} = \dfrac{4a^2}{3}$.

power: Exponential terms which are raised to a further power results in the products of the two **indices**.
$(a^3b^2)^4 = a^{3 \times 4}b^{2 \times 4} = a^{12}b^8$
See also **index notation: fractional index, negative index** and **zero index**, previous page.

indices Plural of **index**.

indivisible A whole number that is not able to be divided by another whole number, other than 1. **Prime numbers** are indivisible as they have no factor other than themselves and one.

inequality A statement that one quantity is larger or smaller than another. The symbols >, <, ≠ are used.

inequality signs The symbols (>, ≥, <, ≤, ≠, ≯, ≱, ≮, ≰), greater than (>), greater than or equal to (≥), less than (<), less than or equal to (≤), not equal to (≠), not greater than (≯), not greater than or equal to (≱), not less than (≮), not less than or equal to (≰).

Inequalities on the number plane Define a region on the number plane.

Q Show $2x + 3y < 6$ on the number plane.
A Draw the line for $2x + 3y = 6$, dash the line to show the inequality. As (0, 0) satisfies the inequality shade the region with (0, 0) included. Note: If it did not then shade the other side.

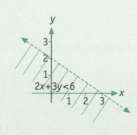

inequation

inequation An algebraic relationship using inequality signs. The solution is a set of values.

> **Q** Graph the inequality $3x + 7 > 12$.
> **A** $3x + 7 > 12$ gives $3x > 5$ and thus $x > \frac{5}{3}$. This result can be graphed on the number line.

inequation, linear See **linear inequation**.

infer Make a predictive statement or state a conclusion, based on observation or reasoning.

infinite Of unlimited size or value. Not countable. Also see **finite**.
The stars in the sky are infinite. The set of natural numbers $N = \{1, 2, 3, ...\}$ is an example of an infinite set.

infinity (Symbol ∞). This is a concept not a value. No matter how great the number or distant the point there is another number larger or point further away. The sequence $1, 2, 3, 4, 5, ...$ is infinite as there is no end value.

inscribe To construct one figure inside another.
The vertices touch an enclosed figure.
See also **incircle** and **circumcircle**.

insert An instruction: To put in a sign or an **operation**.

integers Signed whole numbers. An infinite set of numbers.
Represented by the letters J or Z.
$$... -3, -2, -1, 0, +1, +2, +3, ...$$

integers, on the number line: Note: only the marked values are integers. There are gaps between each integer.

intercept The point where a graph crosses an *axis*.

intercept form Of the straight line. $y = mx + b$, where b is the y-intercept. Also $y = mx + c$, where c is the y-intercept.

interest The payment made for the use of money invested (or borrowed).
Compound: See **compound interest**.
Simple: See **simple interest**.

interior The inside of something.

interior angles The angles inside a shape.

Interior angles of a triangle.

Opposite interior angle.

interpolate To calculate or estimate a value between two other numbers, already known or within a graph.

Q Estimate the temperature at 2:30 pm when it is 23°C at 2pm and 27°C at 3pm.

A As 2:30 is mid way, find the mean of the two temperatures:
$\frac{23 + 27}{2} = \frac{50}{2} = 25$. Thus the interpolated temperature would be 25°C.

inter-quartile range (IQR) A statistical **measures of spread** or **dispersion**. Found as the difference between the first quartile (25th **percentile**) and the third **quartile** (75th percentile). See these entries.

```
1  3 | 4  7  11  17 | 20  21     IQR = Q₃ – Q₁
     3.5            18.5              = 18.5 – 3.5
     Q₁             Q₃                = 15
```

Intersect To cross each other.

AB intersects CD at E.

Line AB intersects the circle at C and D.

intersecting lines Lines in the same plane that are not parallel.

AC and BD intersect at K.

intersecting chords See **chord**, and **circle, intersecting chords and secants**.

intersecting secants See **secants**, and **circle, intersecting chords and secants**.

intersection (∩) The elements that belong to two sets. The region formed in a Venn diagram where the two sets overlap; the common region. See also **Venn diagram**.

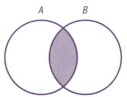

Intersection Venn diagram.
The shaded region is $A \cap B$.

intersection of graphs The points of intersection of two graphs can be found by drawing the graphs or by **algebraic** methods through the use of simultaneous equations. Always check by the substitution of these values into the equations. See **simultaneous equations**.

Note: The algebraic method involves substitution into the higher order equation from the **linear equation**.
$y = 4x^2$ and $y = x + 3$ gives $4x^2 = x + 3 \Rightarrow 4x^2 - x - 3 = 0$ which factorises as $(4x + 3)(x - 1) = 0$ and the result $x = -\frac{3}{4}$ or $x = 1$ follows.

intersection of linear inequations Represented on the number plane by the overlap of two half planes defined by the **linear inequations**.

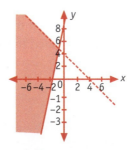

interval 1 The straight line join of two points.
length (distance between two points):
Given by the formula $d = \sqrt{(x_2 - x_1)^2 + (y_2 - y_1)^2}$

> **Q** Find the distance between $A(3, -4)$ and $B(5, 8)$.
> **A** $d = \sqrt{(x_2 - x_1)^2 + (y_2 - y_1)^2}$
> $= \sqrt{(5 - 3)^2 + (8 - -4)^2}$
> $= \sqrt{(2)^2 + (12)^2}$
> $= \sqrt{148}$
> $= 2\sqrt{37}$

midpoint 1: The coordinates of the midpoint of the join of $A(x_1, y_1)$ and $B(x_2, y_2)$ are $\left(\dfrac{x_1 + x_2}{2}, \dfrac{y_1 + y_2}{2}\right)$

> **Q** Find the coordinates of the midpoint of AB, given $A(3, -4)$ and $B(5, 8)$.
> **A** $\left(\dfrac{x_1 + x_2}{2}, \dfrac{y_1 + y_2}{2}\right) = \left(\dfrac{3 + 5}{2}, \dfrac{-4 + 8}{2}\right)$
> $= (4, 2)$

midpoint 2: The time between two events.

> **Q** Find the length of the interval between the end of the first act at 8:18 pm and the beginning of the second act at 8:40 pm.
> **A** The interval is 8:40 – 8:18 = 22 min.

interview A method of **data** collection. Done either in person or by telephone. Questions need to be carefully prepared and a range of answers provided that can be graded (good, poor, bad etc). See also **questionnaire**.

invariance The property of not changing under a process such as a **transformation**. See this entry also.

inverse An element combined with its inverse gives the identity under the operation.

additive: Also called the opposite. The additive inverse of a value is that value with the opposite sign (+ or –). The sum of a number and its additive inverse is zero. +6 is the additive inverse of –6. Thus +6 + –6 = 0.

multiplicative: Often just called the inverse. The multiplicative inverse of a value is the reciprocal of that value. The product of a number and its inverse is 1. $\frac{4}{3}$ is the multiplicative inverse of $\frac{3}{4}$. Thus $\frac{3}{4} \times \frac{4}{3} = 1$.
3 is the multiplicative inverse of $\frac{1}{3}$. Thus $3 \times \frac{1}{3} = 1$.

inverse functions A function that reverses the original function. Symbol f^{-1}. For the function $f(x) = 5x - 1$, the inverse function is found by interchanging the **dependent** and **independent variables** and then rewriting the equation. Use $y = f(x)$.
$y = 5x - 1 \Rightarrow 5x = y + 1 \Rightarrow x = \frac{y+1}{5}$. Thus the inverse function is $f^{-1}(x) = \frac{x+1}{5}$.

inverse operation The operation that reverses the original operation. **Addition** and **subtraction**, **multiplication** and **division**, and **powers** and **roots** are all inverse operations to each other.

inverse variation (or proportion) $y = \frac{k}{x}$ or $xy = k$, where k is a constant. Other examples include $y = \frac{k}{x^2}$ and $y = \frac{k}{\sqrt{x}}$: Indicates the relationship between two variables is such that as the value of one variable increases the other decreases. Thus as one variable increases the other decreases and vice versa. The product of the two values remains constant. The variables are related inversely. See also **direct variation (or proportion)** and **part(ial) variation**.

For $y = \frac{k}{x}$, as x increases, y decreases and vice versa. At the same time $xy = k$.

This means; y varies inversely as x or y is inversely proportional to x.

invert, to To reverse the numerator and denominator of a fraction. More correctly called the multiplicative inverse. The inverse of a whole number is a fraction with 1 as the numerator and the number as the denominator.

> **Q** Give the inverse of: $\frac{3}{5}$, 4 and $\frac{1}{5}$.
> **A** The inverse of $\frac{3}{5}$ is $\frac{5}{3}$, the inverse of 4 is $\frac{1}{4}$ and the inverse of $\frac{1}{5}$ is 5.

inversion See **invert, to**, above.

investigation The exploration of a situation or context.

investment A purchase or **loan** made for the purpose of deriving additional **income**. See also **interest**.

irrational numbers Numbers that can not be written as a rational number (fraction). A number that can not be expressed as $\frac{a}{b}$, $b \neq 0$ and $a, b \in J$. (J is the set of **integers**)
Examples include $\sqrt{2}$, π, e.

irregular When a figure has sides of unequal length or a pattern does not have regularity. Note: A **regular** figure also has equal angles. See this entry also.

isometric dot paper See **isometric grid paper**, next page.

isometric drawing A drawing using **isometric grid paper** which shows three-dimensional (3D) figures drawn from one corner.

isometric grid paper Grid paper where the three lines are at 120° to each other that make equilateral triangles. The paper enables the drawing of three-dimensional (3D) diagrams. It can be used to show transformations in three dimensions. See also **isometric drawing**.

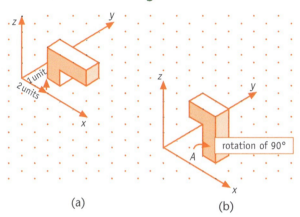

(a) (b)

isometric transformations Transformations where lengths, angles and area are unchanged. Literally; *the same measure.* **Reflection**, **rotation** and **translation** are examples. See these separate entries. See also **non-isometric transformations**.

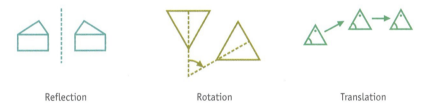

Reflection Rotation Translation

isosceles triangle A triangle with two sides equal. The two angles at the base of the equal sides are also equal.

isosceles trapezium   A **trapezium** where two opposite sides that are not parallel are equal in length.

iteration   The process of repeated operations to approach or reach a solution to an **equation**.

> **Q** Find an estimate of $\sqrt{3}$ by iteration.
> **A** To find $\sqrt{3}$, take an estimate of 1.5. Divide 3 by 1.5 to give 2.
> The next estimate is $\frac{1.5 + 2}{2} = 1.75$.
> Now repeat the steps for a second estimate and so on for as many places as required.

j The letter used to represent signed whole numbers, or an infinite set of numbers (integers). The letter z is also used. See **integers**.

Join A connection.

Join A to B.

Join the points A, B, C and D to make a quadrilateral.

joint variation (jointly proportional) When we say that z is jointly proportional to a set of **variables**, it means that z is directly proportional to each variable, taken one at a time.

If z varies jointly with respect to x and y, the equation will be the form $z = kxy$ (where k is a constant).

equation: $c = 5ab$

Variable c is jointly proportional to a and b. That means c is directly proportional to both a and b.

Doubling a causes c to double.

Doubling b causes c to double.

Doubling both a and b causes c to quadruple.

a	b	c
1	1	5
2	1	10
1	2	10
2	2	20

See also **direct variation (or proportion)**, **inverse variation (or proportion)** and **part(ial) variation**.

K k

k Symbol for **kilo**. See this entry, below.

Karnaugh map Also known as a Veitch diagram (K-map or KV-map for short). A diagram consisting of a small number of non-overlapping (mutually exclusive) rectangles used to indicate the relationships between elements of a set and given properties or attributes. Invented in 1953 by Maurice Karnaugh, a telecommunications engineer.

The diagram below illustrates the correspondence between the Karnaugh map and the truth table for the general case of a two-variable problem.

A	B	I
0	0	a
0	1	b
1	0	c
1	1	d

Truth table

	A	
B	0	1
0	a	c
1	b	d

F
Karnaugh map

kB Symbol for **kilobyte**. See this entry.

kb Symbol for **kilobit**. See this entry.

key A means to show information in a graph or statistical display.

```
0 | 1 1 2 5
1 | 2 3 3 4
2 | 1 2 2 4 5 7
3 | 1 4 7
4 | 5 9

2 | 1  represents  21
4 | 5  represents  45
```

kg The symbol for kilogram

kilo (k) A prefix meaning one thousand. Used for units of measure in the SI system. **kB (kilobyte); Kb (kilobit); kg (kilogram); kL (kilolitre); km (kilometre); kt (kilotonne)**, etc. See separate entries.

kilogram (kg)

kilobit (kb) A unit of information, in the **binary number system** equal to 1000 **bits**.

kilobytes (kB) A computer science unit for storage measurement, equal to 1000 **bytes**. 1000 bytes = 1 kB.

kilogram (kg) The base **SI** unit of mass, equal to one thousand grams.
1000 g = 1 kg

kilojoule (kJ) The **SI** unit for energy or work.

kilolitre (kL) An **SI** unit of capacity, equal to 1000 litres.
1000 L = 1 kL

kilometre (km) An **SI** unit of length, equal to one thousand metres.
1000 m = 1 km

kite A quadrilateral with two pairs of adjacent sides equal. The **square** and **rhombus** are special kites.

area of: The area of a kite is the same as the area of a rhombus: Half the product of the lengths of the diagonals. $A = \frac{1}{2}ab$

K km/h, km.h⁻¹

kJ The symbol for **kilojoule**. See this entry, previous page.

kL The symbol for **kilolitre**. See this entry, previous page.

km The symbol for **kilometre**. See this entry, previous page.

km/h, km.h⁻¹ The symbols for kilometres per hour, used to indicate speed. See also **rate**.

kn Symbol for knot. The measure of speed at sea, equal to travelling one **nautical mile** per hour. 20 kn is approximately 37 km/h.

Königsburg bridge problem A problem that stimulated the early study of **networks** and ultimately **topology**. Relates to seven bridges on the Pregel river at the town of Königsburg in Germany. **Euler** proved the task to be impossible. *Can a person start at any point and walk over every bridge only once and end at the starting point?*

kurtosis The measure of the shape of a frequency curve used in statistics. A measure of 'peakedness'.

Positive kurtosis
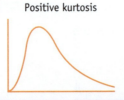

Negative kurtosis
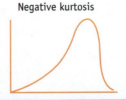

L **1** The symbol for litre. This symbol breaks the rule of only using capital letters for SI units named after people (**Celsius**, Joule, etc). It is written as a capital letter to avoid confusion with the numeral 1.
2 In **Roman numerals** L represents 50.

label To add a name to an object to identify it. The name of an object or axis in a graph.

latitude The position North or South of the **Equator** measured in degrees. Lines of latitude are parallel circles of decreasing radius when moving from the equator to the poles. Their centres are all on the axis of the Earth.
See also **longitude**.

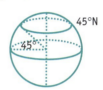

lattice Equal lengths arranged in two parallel rows, one overlapping the other and joined at the intersections. Often made from wood and used to support plants.
See also **Chinese lattice**.

lattice diagram A two-dimensional table used to show results for **probability experiments** that involve two trials. An example would be the listing of outcomes when two six-sided dice are rolled together. See also **array**.

lay-by A method of purchase where goods are retained by the seller until all instalments that add to the **selling price** are paid, usually without interest.

LCD See **lowest common denominator**.

LCM See **lowest common multiple**.

L leading digit

leading digit The first non-zero digit from the left of a number is called the leading digit.

> **Q** Give the leading digits in: 147, 0.004 53.
> **A** In 147, the leading digit is 1. In 0.004 53, the leading digit is 4.

leading digit (estimation) Round off each number involved to its leading figure and then perform the operation.

> **Q** Use leading digit estimation to give a value for 349 × 1750.
> **A** To estimate 349 × 1750, we round to 300 × 2000, which gives 600 000.
> Note: The actual answer is 610 750.

leading figure See **leading digit**, above.

leap year A year of 366 days which occurs once every 4 years. February has 29 days rather than the normal 28. If the year number is divisible by 4 it is a leap year. Century years must be divisible by 400 to be a leap year.
2000 is a leap year while 2100 is not.
The Olympic Games are held in a leap year.

least The smallest amount or quantity in a group.

least squares method Used with a **graphics calculator** to find the line of regression. It involves finding a line that minimises the sum of the squares of the vertical deviations of each data point to the **regression line**.

LinReg(a + bx)
L_1, L_2, Y_1

length The distance from one end to the other. See also **width**, **depth**, **breadth**.

length, measurement of The measurement of length involves using standardised measurements such as the metre and its subdivisions (cm, mm) and multiples (km).

estimation: Involves a mental comparison of a concept of a measurement (such as length) with an actual measurement (length). This is an example of where practice improves performance.

units of: In the metric system the main units of measurement are millimetre (mm), centimetre (cm), metre (m), kilometre (km). See separate entries.

less than (<) A relationship where the number or quantity to the left of the symbol is smaller than that to the right.
Examples: –7 < –4 and 1 < 4.

less than or equal to (≤) A relationship where the value to the left is smaller than, or equal to, the value to the right of the symbol.
Examples: –7 ≤ –4, –4 ≤ –4 and 6 ≤ 8.

level of accuracy How approximate a value is. See also accuracy and accurate.

lie on a line, to A point lies on a line when the x and y values of the point make the equation of the line true.

> **Q** Determine whether (2, 5) lies on the line with equation $2x - 3y + 11 = 0$.
> **A** $2x - 3y + 11 = 0$ becomes $2 \times 2 - 3 \times 5 + 11 = 0$.
> Thus the point lies on the line.

L light year

light year The distance travelled in one year at the speed of light. It is approximately 9.46×10^{12} km.

like surd Surds that have the same **surd** parts.
$\sqrt{5}$, $3\sqrt{5}$ and $\sqrt{20} = 2\sqrt{5}$ are all like surds.

like terms Terms where the **pronumerals** are exactly the same, including any indices. These like terms can then be collected to simplify the expression.

> **Q** Simplify by collecting like terms: $3x - 5y + y^2 - 4y + 11x - 3y^2$.
> **A** $3x + 11x - 5y - 4y + y^2 - 3y^2$ gives $14x - 9y - 2y^2$.

limit Tending to a value. An example is how a **hyperbola** approaches but does not reach its **asymptotes**. See these entries also.
$1 + \frac{1}{2} + \frac{1}{4} + \frac{1}{8} \ldots$ has a limiting value of 2.

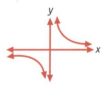

limit of accuracy See **accuracy**.

line An **infinite** collection of points, with length but no width. Usually referring to a straight line, a line can also be curved.

line graphs Graphs drawn on the coordinate axes (number plane) using straight line segments to joint plotted points. A typical line graph is the graph of temperature against time for hourly readings.

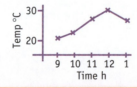

L line of good fit or line of best fit

line of good fit, or line of best fit An attempt to draw a line that shows the relationship between two **variables** in a **scatter diagram**. This is done by attempting to have the same number of points above the line as below the line. See also **regression line**.

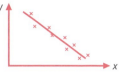

line of reflection The line about which a mirror image is produced. See **line of symmetry**, below.

line of sight The straight line from the eye of the observer to the object.

line of symmetry The line that gives midpoints between an object and an image. See **reflection**.

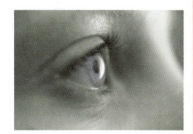

line plot See **dot**, **plot**.

line segment Part of a straight line. A measurable length.

AB is a line segment

linear A straight line, or following a straight path. See **linear equation**, below.

linear graphs The graphs of **linear equations**, see below.

linear equation The equation of a straight line. The **independent** and **dependent** variables both have degree of one. Linear equations have the form $ax + by + c = 0$.
Note: Higher powers for the dependent or independent variables will result in a curve.
For example: $y = x^2$, $x^2 = 4ay$. See also **gradient-intercept form of the equation of a line**.

Excel Junior High School Maths Study Dictionary

L

linear inequations

linear inequations Define a region where the boundary is a straight line defined by a linear graph. The inequation $ax + by + c > 0$ has a dotted boundary and $ax + by + c \geq 0$ has a solid boundary. The region defined by the inequation is known as a half plane.

Rules: $y \geq mx + b$. Draw a solid line and shade above.
$y > mx + b$. Draw a broken (dotted) line and shade above.
$y \leq mx + b$. Draw a solid line and shade below.
$y < mx + b$. Draw a broken (dotted) line and shade below.

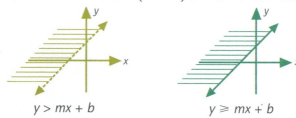

$y > mx + b$ $y \geq mx + b$

linear scale A scale where equal quantities are represented by equal divisions.
Examples: A ruler or a thermometer.

Thermometer in degrees

lines parallel to the axes These have the form $x = h$ (parallel to the *y*-axis) or $y = k$ (parallel to the *x*-axis). The **x-axis** has equation $y = 0$, while the **y-axis** has equation $x = 0$.

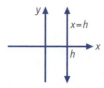 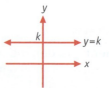

line, number See **number, line**.

lines

concurrent: See **concurrent** lines.
intersecting: See **intersecting** lines.
of symmetry: See **symmetry**.
parallel: See **parallel lines**.
perpendicular: See **perpendicular lines**.
skew: See **skew lines**.

list
An instruction. It means to write out the items in alphabetic or mathematical order. Items are often written one under the other.

> **Q** List 4, 7, 3, 5, 8 in ascending order.
> **A** Ascending order means from smallest to largest.
> Thus the list is 3, 4, 5, 7, 8.

literal equations
Using letters rather than numerals as constants and coefficients in an **algebraic expression**. See also **formulae**.
$y = mx + b$ is a literal equation, the intercept form of the straight line.

litre (L)
A measure of capacity. Used to measure liquids. Has a direct relationship with **volume**. For water at standard temperature and pressure 1 L is the same as 1000 cm^3.
1000 mL = 1 L

loan
Borrowed money to make a purchase that may range from consumer goods, through motor vehicles to houses and business. Interest is charged for the loan of the money and payments made at regular intervals. See **simple interest** and **compound interest**.

location
A description of position with respect to a point of reference. See **number plane**, **coordinates** and **bearings**.

L locus

locus The path traced out by a point moving according to a definite rule after its full range of movement is completed. See also **path**. The plural is loci.

Q Give the locus of a point moving in a plane so that it is a constant distance from a fixed point.
A The locus is a circle, the fixed length is the radius and the fixed point is the centre.

logarithms, common The use of powers (indices) of ten to represent numbers. Developed by **John Napier** to assist with calculations with very large or very small numbers. Originally found by the use of tables, now available on the calculator (log). Note: Bases other than 10 can also be used.
The definition: $\log_b a = c$ means $b^c = a$,
where $a > 0$ and b is a positive real number other than 1.
Example: $\log_{10} 100 = 2$ because $10^2 = 100$ and $\log_2 8 = 3$ because $2^3 = 8$.

logarithmic
graphs: Graphs of the function $f(x) = \log_b x$, with 10 as the most usual base. All logarithmic graphs have the characteristic that they pass through (1, 0) and are asymptotic to the negative y-axis. See **asymptotes**.

scales: Measuring scales that use a logarithm relationship. Used where the value increases very rapidly for a small increase in the independent variable. Examples are the **Richter scale** for measuring earthquakes, **pH** scales to measure acidity and alkalinity and the **decibel** scale for measuring noise.

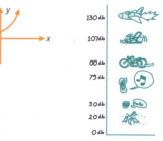

logarithmic, laws: Operations with logarithms operate with **index laws**, as they are indices.
product: $\log_b xy = \log_b x + \log_b y$, $x > 0$ $y > 0$.
The log of a product is the sum of the logs.

quotient: $\log_b \left(\frac{x}{y}\right) = \log_b x - \log_b y$, $x > 0$, $y > 0$.
The log of a quotient is the subtraction of the logs.
power: $\log_b x^p = p \log_b x$
The log of a number raised to a power is the log of the number times the power.
special values: $\log_b 1 = 0$, $\log_b b = 1$, $\log_b b^x = x$

logic Principles of reasoning where one proposition is deduced from other propositions.

logo A computer program that can be used to draw shapes and networks.

long division The algorithm to enable division by divisors of two or more digits. Also used with polynomial division. See **polynomial, division of**.

```
        33
    23)763
        69
        73
        69
         4
```

$763 \div 23 = 33\frac{4}{23}$

longitude The position east or west of the prime meridian, which runs through Greenwich, downstream on the Thames River from the city of London, UK. Measured in degrees. Meridians are all half great circles passing through the north and south poles.

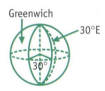

loss A decrease or a move in the negative direction. Defined as: loss = **cost price** – **selling price**. See also **gain**.
I bought the shares for $4.50 and sold for $4.25, a loss of 25 cents per share.

> **Q** Shirts were sold at $15 in a damaged goods sale. If they cost $40, what was the loss?
> **A** loss = cost price – selling price = 40 – 15 = 25
> Thus the loss was $25.

L loss percentage

loss percentage The fraction $\frac{\text{loss}}{\text{cost}}$ converted to a percentage.

Q Shirts were sold at $15 in a damaged goods sale. If they cost $40, what was the loss percentage?

A (from above) = 25

Thus the loss percentage $= \frac{\text{loss}}{\text{cost}} \times 100\%$

$= \frac{25}{40} \times 100$

$= 62.5\%$

lowest common denominator (LCD) The smallest multiple of all the denominators in the addition or subtraction operation. See **LCM** also, below.
For $\frac{1}{3} + \frac{3}{4} - \frac{5}{6}$, the LCD is the lowest common multiple of 3, 4 and 6, which is 12.
Thus $\frac{1}{3} + \frac{3}{4} - \frac{5}{6} = \frac{1 \times 4}{12} + \frac{3 \times 3}{12} - \frac{5 \times 2}{12}$

$= \frac{3}{12}$

$= \frac{1}{4}$

lowest common multiple (LCM) The LCM of two numbers is the first multiple of each number that is the same.
For 3 the multiples are: 3, 6, 9, 12, 15, 18, 21, … and for 5 the multiples are: 5, 10, 15, 20, 25, . . . thus by inspection the LCM of 3 and 5 is 15.

lowest terms For fractions. The numerator and denominator have no common factor (other than 1).

Q Write $\frac{12}{16}$ in lowest terms.

A The fraction $\frac{12}{16}$ is $\frac{3}{4}$ in lowest terms.

M

m The symbol for **metre**.

M 1 The symbol for mega.
Example: A megatonne is 1000 tonnes.
2 The symbol in **Roman numerals** for 1000.

m/s The symbol for metres per second, used to indicate **speed**. See also **rate**.

magic square A square arrangement of numbers that add to the same value across, down and diagonally. The most common are 3 by 3.

6	1	8
7	5	3
2	9	4

⑮

16	3	2	13
5	10	11	8
9	6	7	12
4	15	14	1

㉞

magnetic north The direction that the needle of a magnetic **compass** points. Located close to the North Pole. The angle between the two poles is called the angle of declination and is vital for precise navigation.

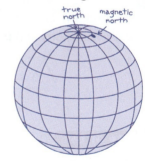

magnitude The size of something. The size of a number without its sign (**absolute value**).
The magnitude of the angle is found by measuring with a **protractor**.

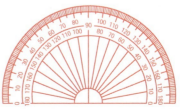

Q Give the magnitude of −4.
A The magnitude of −4 is |−4| = 4.

M major

major The greater; as in major segment. See the entry for **segment of a circle**.

make An instruction: Means to create something.
Make a table to show the following…

many-to-one correspondence A function between two sets where one element in the **domain** is mapped to one element in the **range**, however more than one element in the domain can be mapped to the same element in the range. See also **mapping**, below.
Example: Students (domain) and their heights (range) as more than one student can have the same height.

map See **topological map**.

mapping The process of relating one set of points or values (**domain**) with another set (**co-domain**). Used in the transformations: **reflection**, **rotation** and **translation** and in **relations** and **functions**.

marginal rate of tax The rate of tax applied to any amount above the current taxable **income**.

mark-down When the price is decreased. This is usually expressed as a percentage of the **cost price**. See also **discount**.

mark-up When a price is increased. This is usually expressed as a percentage. See also **profit**.

mass The measurement of the amount of matter in an object. Mass does not change with gravity whereas weight does and weight is the quantity commonly measured by the use of scales. The **SI** unit of mass is the **kilogram**.

mathematical symbols See **symbols in mathematics**.

maximum The greatest quantity or value in a set or in a **region**. For {1, 4, 7, 3, 8, 12, 4, 11} 12 is the maximum value.

maximum value of parabola A **parabola** has a maximum value if the equation has a negative coefficient for the x^2 term. The value is found by finding the **axis of symmetry** of the parabola. $x = -\frac{b}{2a}$, when $y = ax^2 + bx + c$ and substituting this value into the original equation ($a < 0$).

> **Q** Find the maximum value of $y = -3x^2 + 7x - 3$.
>
> **A** For $y = -3x^2 + 7x - 3$, $x = -\frac{7}{2 \times -3}$
> $= \frac{7}{6}$.
>
> Thus $y = -3 \times \left(\frac{7}{6}\right)^2 + 7 \times \frac{7}{6} - 3$
> $= 1\frac{1}{12}$.
>
> Thus the maximum is $1\frac{1}{12}$ and the coordinates of the maximum point are $\left(1\frac{1}{6}, 1\frac{1}{12}\right)$.

M maze

maze A puzzle that has as its solution the finding of a path from beginning to end through a confusing network of lines and gateways.

Maze diagram

mean Used in **statistics**. The average of the scores. See also **measures of central tendency** (below). Represented by $\bar{x}$.

For the scores 1, 1, 1, 2, 4, 5, 7, 7, 9, 10, the mean
$$= \frac{1+1+1+2+4+5+7+7+9+10}{10} = 4.7$$

For grouped data the weighted mean is calculated using the frequencies

x	1	2	3	4	5	6
f	2	5	7	6	3	1

$$\bar{x} = \frac{\Sigma fx}{n} = \frac{1\times 2 + 2\times 5 + 3\times 7 + 4\times 6 + 5\times 3 + 6\times 1}{24} = 3.25$$

measurement The comparison of a characteristic of something with a standard. A form of **data** collection. **Examples:**

Length with a metre   Area with m²
Mass with a kilogram   Volume with m³
Time with an hour   Capacity with a litre.

measure of centre See **measures of central tendency**, below.

measures of central tendency The statistical values that assess the tendency for data to cluster near the middle scores. The values are **mean**, **median** and **mode**. See these entries.

measures of spread

measures of spread The statistical values that asses the tendency for data to be distributed about the central values. The values are **interquartile range**, **range**, **percentiles**, and **standard deviation**. See these entries.

median A **statistics** term. The middle score when the scores are ordered from smallest to largest or largest to smallest. It is also the 50th **percentile**. A **measure of central tendency**.

median of a triangle The line joining the midpoint of the side of a triangle to the opposite **vertex**. See also **centroid of a triangle**.

medicare levy A taxation surcharge calculated as a percentage of **taxable income**. See also **percentage calculations**. Currently $1\frac{1}{2}$% of taxable income.

megalitre (ML) 1000 litres. See also **M** and **litre**.

mensuration The measurement of lengths, areas and volumes.

mensuration formulas Define the measure of one quantity as a function of other quantities.
Examples: **Circle** ($A = \pi r^2$), **rectangle** ($A = lw$), **triangle** $\left(A = \frac{1}{2}bh\right)$, **trapezium** $\left(A = \frac{a + b}{2} \times h\right)$. See these entries also.

meridian of longitude See **longitude**.

metre (m) The basic **SI** measure of length.
1 m = 100 cm = 1000 mm

Excel Junior High School Maths Study Dictionary 177

M metric system

metric system   The decimal system of weights and measures. Formally named the **SI system**. Used for measuring, among others, **length** (m), **mass** (kg), **capacity** (L), **temperature** (°C), **time** (h), **area** (m^2) and **volume** (m^3) as well as derived units. See **SI** also.

The most commonly used divisions are:
milli $\left(\frac{1}{1000}\right)$, centi $\left(\frac{1}{100}\right)$, deci $\left(\frac{1}{10}\right)$,
deca (× 10), hecto (× 100) and kilo (× 1000).

micro μ   A prefix meaning one millionth part.

1 microgram = $\frac{1}{1\,000\,000}$ g = 0. 000 001g.

midday   1200 hours or noon.
The division between am and pm.

midnight   2400 hours.
The division between pm and am.

midpoint   The point in the middle of a set of values or an **interval**.

midpoint of an interval   See **interval, midpoint**.

mile   An **imperial** unit of length measurement. Approximately 1609 m.

millennium One thousand years.
In our calendar, 1 to 1000 was the first millennium. 1001 to 2000 the second. Thus the third millennium started in 2001.

milli A prefix for one thousandth. A millimetre (mm) is one thousandth of a metre.

milligram One thousandth of a gram.
1000 mg = 1 g

millilitre One thousandth of a litre.
1000 mL = 1 L

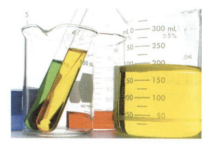

millimetre One thousandth of a metre.
1000 mm = 1 m

million One thousand thousands.
1 000 000 = 10^6

minimum The least quantity in a set of values or the lowest point in a *region*.

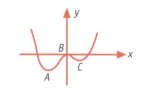

The minimum occurs at point *A*.

M minimum value of parabola

minimum value of parabola A parabola has a minimum value if the equation has a positive **coefficient** for the x^2 term. The value is found by finding the **axis of symmetry** of the parabola.
$x = -\dfrac{b}{2a}$, when $y = ax^2 + bx + c$ and substituting this value into the original equation ($a > 0$).

Q Find the minimum value of $y = 3x^2 - 8x - 3$.

A For $y = 3x^2 - 8x - 3$, $x = -\dfrac{-8}{2 \times 3} = \dfrac{4}{3}$.

Thus $y = 3 \times \left(\dfrac{4}{3}\right)^2 - 8 \times \dfrac{4}{3} - 3 = -8\dfrac{1}{3}$.

Thus the minimum is $-8\dfrac{1}{3}$ and the coordinates of the minimum point are $\left(1\dfrac{1}{3}, -8\dfrac{1}{3}\right)$.

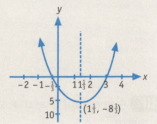

minuend A number from which another number is to be subtracted.
   63   –   17   =   46
minuend – subtrahend = difference

minor The smaller; as in minor segment or minor sector. See the entries for **segment** and **sector**.

minus An instruction: Means to take away, to subtract.

Q Find seven minus four.
A Seven minus four is 3 (7 – 4 = 3).

minute **1** A measurement of time (min).
One sixtieth part of an hour.
2 A measurement of an angle.
One sixtieth part of a degree.

See also **time**, **angle**, **hour** and **second**.

mirror image See **reflection**.

mixed numbers (numerals)

mixed numbers (numerals) Numbers that are a combination of a whole number and a fraction. They can be converted to an **improper fraction**. $3\frac{2}{3} = 3 + \frac{2}{3}$ is a mixed number. It is equal to $\frac{11}{3}$, an improper fraction.

mixed number operations

Addition: Add the **whole numbers** and then separately add the fractions.

Q Add $2\frac{1}{3}$ and $1\frac{2}{5}$.
A $2\frac{1}{3} + 1\frac{2}{5} = 2 + 1 + \frac{1}{3} + \frac{2}{5} = 3 + \frac{5 + 6}{15} = 3\frac{11}{15}$

Division: Convert to **improper fractions** and then invert and multiply.

$3\frac{3}{4} \div 1\frac{2}{3} = \frac{15}{4} \div \frac{5}{3} = \frac{15}{4} \times \frac{3}{5} = \frac{9}{4} = 2\frac{1}{4}$

Multiplication: Convert to improper fractions and then multiply.

$2\frac{3}{4} \times 1\frac{1}{3} = \frac{11}{4} \times \frac{4}{3} = \frac{11}{3} = 3\frac{2}{3}$

Subtraction: Subtract the whole number and then separately subtract the fraction. Advantage can be taken of **directed number operations**.

$4\frac{1}{3} - 2\frac{3}{5} = 2\frac{1}{3} - \frac{3}{5} = 2 + \frac{1 \times 5 - 3 \times 3}{15} = 2 + \frac{-4}{15} = 1\frac{11}{15}$

or $4\frac{1}{3} - 2\frac{3}{5} = 1 + 1\frac{1}{3} - \frac{3}{5} = 1 + \frac{4}{3} - \frac{3}{5} = 1 + \frac{20 - 9}{15} = 1\frac{11}{15}$

See also **calculator use, to convert mixed numbers to improper fractions and return**.

mL The symbol for **millilitre**.

Möbius Strip A surface with only one side. Made by giving a strip of paper a half twist and joining the ends. Named after the German mathematician August Ferdinand Möbius, 1790-1868.

M modal class

modal class The most frequent class in grouped data (see **data, grouped**).
Used with a **frequency distribution table**. The modal class in this table is 31–40.

x	1–10	11–20	21–30	31–40	41–50
f	7	15	21	24	12

mode A statistics term. The most common or most frequently occurring score. A measure of **central tendency**.
For the scores: 1, 3, 3, 5, 7, 9, 12; 3 is the mode
For the scores: 1, 3, 3, 5, 7, 7, 12; both 3 and 7 are modes. This data is **bimodal**. See this entry also.

model A three-dimensional (3D) representation of an actual or designed object. See also **net of a solid**.

modelling Using mathematical concepts, structures and relationships to describe a situation. Often uses **algebraic equations**.

modern box plot A form of box plot where the **outlier** is separately shown.

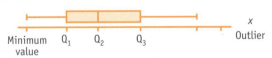

See **box-and-whiskers diagram**.

modulus The absolute value of a number. See **absolute value**.

money See **currency, decimal**.

month

month Part of the arrangement of the calendar into months and days.

The months of the calendar and the days in each are: January (31), February (28 or 29), March (31), April (30), May (31), June (30), July (31), August (31), September (30), October (31), November (30) and December (31). See *year* and also *leap year*.

monthly An event that occurs each calendar month such as the payment of rent or the repayment of a *loan*.
The payments occur monthly on the 15th.

more The greater of two amounts or quantities.
Peter has 15 and Jon has 18. This means Jon has more than Peter.

most The greatest of more than two amounts or quantities.
Of the numbers −8, 2 and 5, 5 is the greatest.
Of the buckets containing 5 L, 7 L and 9 L, the 9 L bucket contains the most water.

multiple When two numbers are multiplied together.
2, 4, 6 are the first three multiples of 2.
24 is a multiple of 2, 3, 4, 6, 8 and 12.
See also *lowest common multiple (LCM)*.

M multiples

multiples Numbers that are the product of two integers.
3, 6, 9, 12, . . . are all multiples of 3.

multilateral To have many sides.

multiplicand The number that is to be multiplied.
$17 \times 4 = 68$.
multiplicand × multiplier = product.

multiplication × The shortened form of repeated addition.
$3 + 3 + 3 + 3 + 3 + 3 = 6 \times 3 = 18$.   *This is 6 lots of 3.*

by algebraic fractions: The operation uses the same method as numeric fractions. After **cancelling**, multiply the numerators for the new numerator and separately multiply the denominators to produce the new denominator.
$$\frac{3a}{5} \times \frac{20b}{9} = \frac{4ab}{3}$$

by one: When a number is multiplied by one the result is the original number. One is called the **identity element** for multiplication.

of decimals: The decimal points are ignored and the multiplication completed. The number of places after decimal points is then counted and the answer has that many **decimal places**.
3.25×1.7 becomes $325 \times 17 = 5525$. Three places of decimals are necessary thus the answer is 5.525

of directed numbers: Like signs give a positive (+),
while unlike signs give a negative (–).
$-3 \times -4 = +12 = 12$ $+3 \times +4 = 3 \times 4 = 12$
$+3 \times -4 = 3 \times -4 = -12$ $-3 \times 4 = -12$

of fractions: Multiply the numerators to produce the new numerator and the denominators to produce the new denominator. See also **cancelling** and **mixed numerals**.
$$\frac{5}{9} \times \frac{3}{8} = \frac{5}{24}$$

of indices: To multiply terms with the same base, add the indices.
$$2^3 \times 2^4 = 2^{3+4}$$
$$= 2^7$$
$$3a^4b \times 7a^4b^5 = 3 \times 7a^{4+4}b^{1+5}$$
$$= 21a^8b^6$$

of pronumerals: We multiply the numerals together and then the pronumerals, without multiplication signs. See also **multiplication, of indices**, above.
$$5abc \times 3ac \times 4bc = 5 \times 3 \times 4a^2b^2c^3$$
$$= 60a^2b^2c^3$$

of surds: Multiply the whole numbers and separately multiply the surds.
$$\sqrt{3} \times \sqrt{5} = \sqrt{3 \times 5}$$
$$= \sqrt{15}$$
$$2\sqrt{3} \times 5\sqrt{6} = 2 \times 5\sqrt{3 \times 6}$$
$$= 10\sqrt{18}$$
$$= 10 \times 3\sqrt{2}$$
$$= 30\sqrt{2}$$

multiplier A number by which the multiplicand is multiplied. See **multiplicand**.

multiply To carry out the process of **multiplication**, see previous page.

mutually exclusive events Events that can not happen at the same time. To calculate the probability of the joint event, add the separate probabilities. See **probability** also.
Selecting a piece of fruit from 8 apples, 6 oranges and 5 bananas.
$Pr(\text{apple or orange}) = \frac{8}{19} + \frac{6}{19} = \frac{14}{19}$.

N name

name An instruction to describe something, usually a figure such as a triangle or quadrilateral, often using the letters on a diagram.
Name the angle θ in the diagram. θ is BÂE.

nano A prefix which is one thousand millionth.
This is $= \dfrac{1}{1\,000\,000\,000} = 10^{-9} = 0.000\,000\,001$.

Napier, John Scottish mathematician, 1550–1617, mainly remembered for his development of **logarithms**. He also invented a set of rods, called Napier's Bones, used as an aid to calculation. They were based on a **logarithmic scale**.

Naperian logarithms See **natural logarithms**, below and **Napier, John**, above.

natural logarithms (ln) A logarithm using *e* as the base. Written as ln *x* or $\log_e x$.

natural numbers The number 1 and any other number obtained by adding 1 to it repeatedly. Used for ordering and counting: 1, 2, 3, 4, 5, ...

nautical mile The distance on the Earth's surface subtended by one sixtieth of one degree at the centre. As this is a natural unit easily found, it is still used in navigation of ships and aircraft. Equal to approximately 1852 m. One nautical mile per hour is one **knot**.

negative gradient The slope of a line that dips to the right. The line AB has negative gradient.

negative integers (numbers) Integers less than zero. Part of the set of directed numbers. Also see this entry. –1, –2, –3, –4, –5, –6, –7, –8, –9, …
Note: Negative numbers are numbers less than zero (–3.4, –√3 etc).

net of a solid The two-dimensional (2D) layout of the faces of a solid, showing their relationship with one another. Often used to construct a model of the solid.

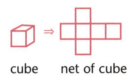

cube   net of cube

net mass The mass of the contents of a package, or the load on a transport vehicle.

net pay or income The amount that an employee receives after all taxes and deductions have been made from the gross pay. See also **gross pay or income**.

network A system of lines or arcs and intersections, called **nodes** or **vertices**, that represent **paths** and their **intersections**. See also **topology** and **Königsberg bridge problem**.

N node

node A point where straight lines or curves meet. See also **network**, previous page.

nominal data A form of categorical data. It contains values which can only be classified by the name or category from which they arise. See also **qualitative data**, **ordinal data** and **categorical data**.
An example is selecting cars by colour.

nonagon A polygon with nine sides.

Regular nonagon   Irregular nonagon

none Nothing. See **zero**.

non-convex A shape where some of the surfaces or sides bend in towards the centre of the shape. See also **concave**.

non-isometric transformations Transformations where lengths or angles are changed. **Enlargement** or **reduction** are examples. See **isometric transformations** also.

non-linear Non-straight line. A curve.

normal At right angles. See **perpendicular**.

normal distribution A distribution curve that is symmetrical about the **mean**, **median** and **mode** that are all represented as the same score.

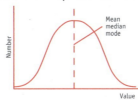

notation, expanded See **expand** and **expanded form**.

not equal (≠) A relationship where two quantities are different in size. See also **greater than** and **less than**.

> **Q** Show a relationship between 8 and −8.
> **A** $8 \neq -8$

nothing None. See **zero**.

nought None. See **zero**.

null hypothesis Used in **statistics** to test an observation. The null hypothesis is that there is no difference between an experimental and a control group.

With fertiliser   Without fertiliser

N number

number The measure of a quantity.
The quantity ∗ ∗ ∗ is represented by 3.
binary: See **binary numbers**.
directed: See **directed numbers**.
line: A representation of the various sets of numbers evenly spaced on a straight line. It can be used to perform **operations** and to graph sets of numbers.

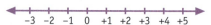

pairs: See **coordinates, rectangular**.
plane: See **coordinates, rectangular**.
patterns: A set of numbers that follow a pattern or rule. See also **figurate numbers**.
for example: The numbers 1, 4, 7, 10, 13 obey the rule $p = 3n - 2$.
plane: An alternative name for the coordinate axes. See **coordinates, rectangular**.
properties: Also known as the laws of **arithmetic**.
1 Multiplying any number by 1 leaves it unchanged. See **unity**.
   $463 \times 1 = 463$.
2 Multiplying any number by zero gives zero. See **zero**.
   $463 \times 0 = 0$.
3 Adding zero to any number leaves it unchanged. See **zero**.
   $463 + 0 = 463$.
4 When adding two numbers the order does not change the answer. See **commutative property (or law) of addition**.
   $3 + 5 = 8 = 5 + 3$.
5 When multiplying two numbers the order of multiplication does not change the answer. See **commutative property (or law) of multiplication**.
   $3 \times 5 = 15 = 5 \times 3$.
6 When adding more than two numbers, the order does not change the answer. See **associative property, addition**.
   $2 + 3 + 4 = 9 = 2 + (3 + 4)$.
7 When multiplying more than two numbers, the order does not change the answer. See **associative property, multiplication**.
   $2 \times 3 \times 4 = 24 = 2 \times (3 \times 4)$.
sentences: An alternative name for an **equation**. See this entry.
whole: See **whole numbers**.

number machine An imaginary device that processes an input number to produce an output number. Used as an introduction to **equations** and **relations**.

number of elements, n(A) The number of elements in the set *A*. *n*(*A* only) indicates the number of elements in the set *A* only. See also **cardinal number**.

number plane See **coordinates, rectangular**.

numbering system A method of writing numerals to indicate different numbers and the rules that go with them. See also **Hindu-Arabic numerals**, **Roman numerals**.

The numbers one to ten in Chinese numerals.

numeral A symbol used to represent a number.
3 represents ∗ ∗ ∗
basic: See **basic numeral**.
Egyptian: See **Egyptian numerals**.
Hindu-Arabic: See **Hindu-Arabic numerals**.
Roman: See **Roman numerals**.

N numeration

numeration A system of symbols used to represent numbers. See **numbers**, previous page.

numerator The top part of a fraction. See also **denominator**.

The fraction $\dfrac{3}{8} \quad \dfrac{\text{numerator}}{\text{denominator}}$

numerical Referring to **numbers**.

numeric(al) data Data where each result is a number. An example is the measurement of height. Numerical data can be **discrete** or **continuous**. See these entries.

numeric fractions See **fraction**.

object See **image** and also **reflection**.

oblique Not **perpendicular** or **parallel**. To lean to one side.

oblique pyramid A pyramid where the axis is not **perpendicular** to the base.

oblique solid A solid that leans when standing on its base.

oblong An alternative name for a **rectangle**. See this entry.

observations Watching, counting and recording events. An example of **data** collection.

obtuse angle An angle greater than 90° and less than 180°.

obtuse-angled triangle A triangle where one angle is **obtuse**, as above. (The other two are obviously acute). See also **acute-angled triangle**.

O o'clock

o'clock Used when telling time as full hours.
The time is nearly five o'clock.

Big Ben, London

octal A number system based on 8. Thus $8_{ten} = 10_{eight}$ as this represents one 8 and no units.

> **Q** Express 23_{eight} as a base 10 numeral.
> **A** $23_{eight} = 2 \times 8 + 3 = 19_{ten}$

octagon An eight-sided **polygon**.

Regular octagon   Irregular octagon

octagonal prism A **prism** whose base is an octagon.

octagonal pyramid A **pyramid** whose base is an octagon.

octahedron A solid with eight triangular faces.

octahedron, regular One of the five **platonic solids**. A solid with eight faces all of which are identical equilateral triangles. See also **tetrahedron**, **cube**, **dodecahedron** and **icosahedron**.

odd numbers Natural numbers not divisible by 2. They are of the form $2n - 1$, where n is a positive integer. All odd numbers end with 1, 3, 5, 7, or 9.
1, 3, 5, 7, 9, 11, 13, 15, . . .

odds A gambling term to indicate the return for an amount wagered. A reverse application of the probability of an event occurring, however not directly. Odds are set so the gambler is at a disadvantage. Odds of 5 to 1 indicate a probability of 1 in 6 when in fact the true probability may be closer to 1 in 10. Odds for outcomes such as a sporting event are purely subjective.
Note: Bookmakers odds and Totaliser Agency Board (TABCorp, a government licensed public company) odds differ. For 5 to 1, a bookmaker pays $5 + $1 for $1 wagered while the TAB pays $5 only.

odometer An instrument that records the distance travelled by a vehicle. Usually located in the speedometer of the vehicle.

of An occasional operation. It means to multiply. In the order of operations it comes after brackets but ahead of division and multiplication.
Note: In senior school and higher mathematics there are many additional uses of of.

Q Find $\frac{2}{3}$ of 4.
A $\frac{2}{3}$ of 4 means $\frac{2}{3} \times 4$.

o ogive

ogive The name often given to the **cumulative frequency polygon**. See this entry. Derived from an architectural term describing an arch in Moorish buildings. Ogive has many other meanings, a number of which are associated with ballistics.

one-dimensional (1D) An object that has only length. A line is an example.

One-dimensional shape (1D)   Two-dimensional shape (2D)

one-to-one correspondence Matching objects one to one in sequence. See also **many-to-one correspondence** and also **domain**, **co-domain** and **range**.
The children were one-to-one in correspondence with their seats in the classroom.

open Without a top. Used with solids to indicate a container.
A shoe box is an open rectangular prism.

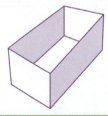

open circle To indicate an inequality on a number line. See also **closed circle** and **inequalities**.

$x < 4$

Note: Includes all real values less than 4, so 4 is not included.

open curve A curve where the beginning and end points are different. See also **closed curve**.

operations A mathematical process combining numbers or sets. See entries for the following:
addition
division
indices
intersection
multiplication
order of
subtraction
union.

opposite angles, vertically See **vertically opposite angles**.

opposite numbers Numbers that add to zero. See **inverse, additive**.

opposite operations Operations that reverse each other. Addition and subtraction; multiplication and division; and powers and roots are significant examples.
Examples: 1 $6 + 5 = 11 \Leftrightarrow 11 - 5 = 6$
2 $6 \times 5 = 30 \Leftrightarrow 30 \div 5 = 6$
3 $\sqrt[3]{8} = 2 \Leftrightarrow 2^3 = 8$

O opposite side

opposite side In trigonometry. The side opposite the angle.

order A relation that describes the location of elements in a set with respect to each other. See also **equality** and **inequalities**.

order of operations The set of rules that give the order in which the operations are performed. See also **brackets** and **power**. When + and − are together they are performed from left to right. Similarly × and ÷.

Brackets	Exponentials	of	÷ and ×	+ and −
B	E	O	DM	AS

order of rotational symmetry The number of times a figure can be rotated about the centre of **rotation** (or point of rotation) to match the original figure to return to the original orientation.
An equilateral triangle has order of rotational symmetry of 3.

ordered pairs An alternative name for (Cartesian) **coordinates**. See this entry. See also **number plane** and **coordinates, rectangular**.

ordered stem-and-leaf plots A refinement of the stem-and-leaf plot where the elements of the leaf entries are placed in increasing order.
See **stem-and-leaf plot (table)**.

ordering Arranging in order according to size, value or number.

198   *Excel Junior High School Maths Study Dictionary*

ordinal data A form of categorical data. Information which can be classified in a similar way as nominal data which can be then placed in order.
See also **categorical data** and **nominal data**.
Example: The ranking of sporting teams in a competition, based on number of wins.

ordinal number A number that shows the position or place of a number.

First	Second	Third
1st	2nd	3rd
1	2	3

ordinate The name of the *y*-axis in the **number plane**. The *y*-coordinate which is the distance from the *x*-axis. See also **abscissa**.

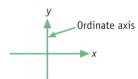

ordinate diagram See **dot, plot**.

origin The beginning. The start of something.
in the number plane: The point where the two axes intersect.

Excel Junior High School Maths Study Dictionary

orthocentre

orthocentre The point where the three altitudes of a triangle intersect. It can be either inside or outside the triangle.

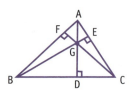 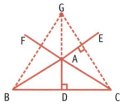

orthogonal Lines or planes that are at right-angles to each other. An alternative name for perpendicular or normal. See **perpendicular**.

orthogonal drawing Shows the true shapes and **dimensions**. Consists of front view, top view and side view of the object.

Object Front Side Top

outcome(s) Possible results for scores in **data** collection.

H H T T T H T H H H   H | T
                         6 | 4

> **Q** In tossing a coin what are the possible outcomes?
> **A** There are two possible outcomes, a head or a tail.

outlier Score or scores that are separated from the main body of scores. A likely outlier is a value that lies more than 1.5 times the **interquartile range** outside of the upper or lower quartiles. This separation is defined for certain types of **data** collection. See also **modern box plot**.

> **Q** Identify the outlier for the data 20, 22, 23, 25, 28 and 40.
> **A** In the data set: 20, 22, 23, 25, 28, 40; 40 is the outlier due to its distance from the other scores.

oval **1** An egg shaped plane figure that is symmetrical about one axis. One end is more pointed than the other.
2 A common name for an *ellipse* which is a regular closed curve.

overtime Payment for work done outside normal hours or for work done over the normal number of hours expected to be worked in a week. Paid at *penalty rates*.

Q Lawrence is paid $485.64 per week for a normal 38 hours work. He receives time-and-a-half for overtime and double time for Sunday work. How much does he receive in gross pay for a 44-hour week where 3 hours are worked on Sunday?

A The hourly rate is 485.64 ÷ 38 = 12.78.
Overtime: 44 − 38 − 3 = 3.
Pay for this overtime = 12.78 × 1.5 × 3
 = 57.51
Sunday: 12.78 × 2 × 3 = 76.68
Gross pay = 485.64 + 57.51 + 76.68
 = 619.83
Thus Lawrence receives $619.83 in gross pay for a 44-hour week.

pair Two things that belong together.
A pair of boots . . .

palindromic numbers Numbers that read the same forwards as backwards.
121   14641   1354531 are examples.

pantograph An instrument used for copying a **plane shape** (such as a map or drawing) onto another plane surface. Often used for **enlargement** or **reduction** of the shape.

parabola The curve which represents a **quadratic equation**.

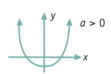

parabola sketching The details needed are axis of symmetry, maximum or minimum value and axes intercepts, see below and on the opposite page.
axis of symmetry: Found by obtaining $x = -\dfrac{b}{2a}$, from the general equation $y = ax^2 + bx + c$.
maximum and minimum values. Found by substituting the x value of the axis of symmetry into the general equation. A maximum value occurs when a is negative and a minimum occurs when a is positive.

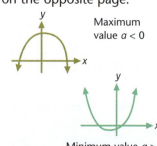

parabola sketching

axes intercepts: x-axis when $y = 0$. y-axis when $x = 0$.

> **Q** Find the axes intercepts for the parabola $y = 3x^2 + 5x + 2$.
> **A** x-axis: For $y = 0$, $3x^2 + 5x + 2 = (3x + 2)(x + 1) = 0$.
> Thus $x = -\frac{2}{3}$ or $x = -1$.
> y-axis: For $x = 0$, $y = 3x^2 + 5x + 2 = 0 + 0 + 2 = 2$.
> See also **quadratic equations**.

sketching parabolas:

Q Sketch the following parabolas:
$y = x^2$, $y = -x^2$, $y = 3x^2$, $y = \frac{1}{3}x^2$, $y = (x + 2)^2$,
$y = (x - 2)^2$, $y = (x - 2)^2 + 2$, $y = -\frac{1}{2}x^2$

A
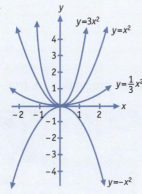
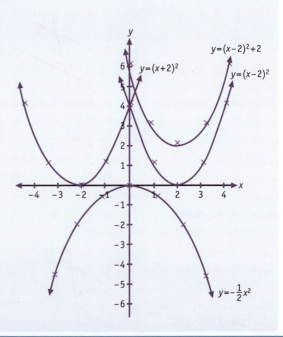

paradox

paradox A self-contradictory statement. One that at first appears logical and then on deeper examination leads to an absurd conclusion. See Achilles and the Tortoise.

parallel The property of being a constant distance apart. Usually refers to lines and planes.

parallel line tests See parallel lines below.

parallel lines

geometric: Lines which are a constant distance apart. They have the same slope. *AB // CD*.

When they are cut by a transversal the following angle properties are true.
Alternate angles are equal.

Also called *z-angles*.
Cointerior angles are supplementary.

$a + b = 180°$

Also called *c-angles*.
Corresponding angles are equal.

Also called *f-angles*.

parallel lines, gradient: Lines are parallel if they have the same gradient. The equations of the lines are examined to find gradients.

Q Show that $2x + 3y = 6$ and $4x + 6y = 8$ are parallel and sketch the lines.

A The gradient form of the straight line is
$y = mx + b$, where m is the gradient.
$2x + 3y = 6$, transforms to $y = -\frac{2}{3}x + 2$ and so $m_1 = -\frac{2}{3}$ and similarly for
$4x + 6y = 8$, $y = \frac{-4x}{6} + \frac{8}{6}$ and so $m_2 = -\frac{4}{6} = -\frac{2}{3}$.
Thus as $m_1 = m_2 = -\frac{2}{3}$, the lines are parallel.

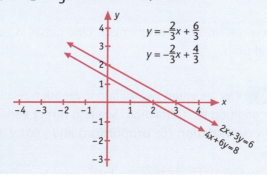

parallelepiped A prism made of **parallelograms**.

parallelogram A **quadrilateral** with opposite sides parallel.

parallelogram properties The opposite sides are equal.

continued over

P parentheses

The opposite angles are equal.

The diagonals bisect.
Rotational symmetry of order two.

parentheses Grouping symbols ( ). Commonly called **brackets**. See these entries.

parsec An **astronomical unit** of measurement. One parsec is equal to 206 265 astronomical units.

part(ial) variation Occurs when two different variation relationships are combined under addition or subtraction. See also **direct variation (or proportion)**, **inverse variation (or proportion)** and **joint variation (jointly proportional)**.

If y varies partly as x and partly as $\frac{1}{x^2}$ then the total variation is expressed as $y = kx + \frac{m}{x^2}$, where k and m are constants.

partition To divide into separate parts which together make the whole. See also **division**. The alphabet can be partitioned into vowels {a, e, i, o, u} and consonants.

Pascal's triangle An ancient concept, studied as early as the year 1000 and developed by Blaise Pascal, French Mathematician, 1623-1662, for use in studies in **algebra** and **probability**. Each new number is generated by the addition of the two above it. The numbers in any row are **combinations** of the number of the row.

```
            1
          1   1
        1   2   1              ²C₀  ²C₁  ²C₂
      1   3   3   1         ³C₀  ³C₁  ³C₂  ³C₃
    1   4   6   4   1
  1   5  10  10   5   1            etc.
```

$^2C_0$ $^2C_1$ $^2C_2$
$^3C_0$ $^3C_1$ $^3C_2$ $^3C_3$
etc.

path A connected set of points. The route or line along which a person, object or point moves according to a set of instructions. See also **locus**.

pattern A repeated design using numbers, letters, objects or shapes or a combination of these. 1, 4, 7, 10, . . . is a number pattern.

pay back method for subtraction More correctly named equal addition method. See the entry for **subtraction, of whole numbers**.

payment by piece See **piecework**.

penalty rates rate of pay for work on an hourly basis that is for **overtime** or outside normal hours (as defined in a pay award or enterprise agreement). Usually at **time-and-a-half** or **double-time**. See these entries.

pendulum A device that swings in a vertical arc about a fixed point. Often used to regulate the movement of a clock.

pentagon A five-sided **polygon**.

pentagonal numbers

pentagonal numbers Numbers that can be represented by a pentagonal pattern of dots. The first five pentagonal numbers are 1, 5, 12, 22 and 35.

pentagonal prism A *prism* with a pentagon as the base.

pentagonal pyramid A *pyramid* with a pentagon as the base.

pentahedron A solid figure with 5 plane faces. A square pyramid is an example.

pentominos Plane shapes made from five equal squares so that at least one whole side is shared. There are 12 in total.

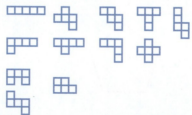

per annum (pa) Each year. Usually quoted with reference to **interest** rates. 15% pa means a rate of 15% for one year.

per cent An abbreviation of Latin for *by the hundred*. The symbol is %. See **percentage**, below.

percentage A **rate** or proportion expressed as part of 100.
Example: $17\% = \frac{17}{100}$, while $\frac{35}{39} = \frac{35}{39} \times 100 = 89.7\%$ (to one decimal place).

decimal conversion:
1 To convert a decimal to a percentage multiply by 100.

Q Convert 0.147 to a percentage.
A $0.147 = 0.147 \times 100$
$= 14.7\%$

2 To convert a percentage to a decimal divide by 100.

Q Convert 37.65% to a decimal.
A $37.65\% = 37.65 \div 100$
$= 0.3765$

fraction conversion:
1 To convert a fraction to a percentage, multiply by 100.

Q Convert $\frac{3}{11}$ to a percentage.
A $\frac{3}{11} = \frac{3}{11} \times 100$
$= 27\frac{3}{11}\%$
$= 27.27\%$ (to 2 decimal places)

2 To convert a percentage to a fraction, write the percentage as the numerator with 100 as the denominator and then simplify the fraction.

Q Write 16.4% as a fraction.
A $16.4\% = \frac{16.4}{100}$
$= \frac{164}{1000}$ ($\times$ by $\frac{10}{10}$)
$= \frac{41}{250}$ (in lowest terms)

continued over

P percentage

mixed number conversion: Write the whole number as hundreds and then convert the fraction part in the normal manner.

> **Q** Convert $1\frac{3}{7}$ to a percentage.
> **A** $1\frac{3}{7} = 100 + \frac{3}{7} \times 100$
> $= \left(100 + 42\frac{6}{7}\right)\%$
> $= 142.86\%$ (to 2 decimal places)

percentage of a quantity: Write the percentage as a decimal and multiply by the quantity.

> **Q** Find 24% of $365.
> **A** 24% of $365 $\Leftrightarrow$ 0.24 × 365 = 87.6, which gives $87.60.

One quantity as a percentage of another: Write the first as a fraction of the second and then multiply by 100. Both quantities must be in the same units.

> **Q** Express 17 cents as a percentage of $5.
> **A** $\frac{17}{500} \times 100 = 3.4\%$. **Note:** The $5 was changed into 500 cents.

percentage, change: See **decrease** and **increase**, below.

composition: The percentages of parts that make up the whole.
The percentage composition of a popular fruit drink is 22% fruit juice and 78% water.

conversion: See **decimal conversion**, and **fractions conversion**, previous page.

decrease: The percentage by which an amount or quantity has decreased. See also **increase**, below.

> **Q** Find the percentage decrease when an item bought for $40 is sold for $36.
> **A** The decrease is $4. Percentage decrease is $\frac{4}{40} \times 100 = 10\%$.

increase: The percentage by which an amount or quantity has increased. See also **decrease**, above.

> **Q** Find the percentage increase when an item bought for $40 is sold for $48.
> **A** The increase is $8. Percentage increase is $\frac{8}{40} \times 100 = 20\%$.

percentage frequency

percentage frequency The percentage value of the **relative frequency**: the fraction made by the frequency of one score over the total of the frequencies.

Q For the data

x	1	2	3	4	5
f	3	5	8	7	2

$\Sigma f = 25$

Calculate the percentage frequency for a score of 3.

A Relative frequency of 3 is $\frac{8}{25}$.

Thus percentage frequency is $\frac{8}{25} \times 100 = 32\%$.

percentage profit See **profit**.

percentile One of the 99 values of a **variable** dividing a set into 100 parts. The 25th percentile is the first **quartile**; 25% of the scores are below or equal to this number. The 75th percentile is the third quartile. The 50th percentile is the **median**. See these entries also.

perfect number A number whose factors, other than itself, total (add) to the number. 6 is perfect as the factors of 6; 1, 2, and 3 add to 6. 28 and 496 are two other perfect numbers.

perfect square

1 Used in **algebra**. When a **binomial** is multiplied by itself.
$(a + b)^2 = a^2 + 2ab + b^2$ and $(a - b)^2 = a^2 - 2ab + b^2$

Q Expand $(3x - 7y)^2$.

A $(3x - 7y)^2 = (3x)^2 - 2 \times 3x \times 7y + (7y)^2$
$= 9x^2 - 42xy + 49y^2$.

2 The square of an integer or rational number.

Examples: $144 = 12^2$ and $\frac{4}{25} = 0.16 = \left(\frac{2}{5}\right)^2$.

perigon
Equal to 360°. Another name for a **revolution**. See this entry also.

perimeter
The **boundary** of a closed shape or curve. Also the distance around a plane shape. Found by adding the lengths of the individual sides. See also **circumference**.
Rectangle: $P = 2(l + w)$. Square: $P = 4s$

> **Q** Find the perimeter of each figure:
> **A** i $P = 2(7 + 3)$
> $\quad\quad = 2 \times 10$
> $\quad\quad = 20$ cm.
> ii $P = 4s$
> $\quad\quad = 4 \times 3$
> $\quad\quad = 12$ cm

periodic
Repeats at regular intervals.
Examples: 0, 1, 2, 0, 1, 2, 0, 1, 2, . . . or a graph of the rise and fall of the tide.

permutation
An ordered arrangement or sequence of a group of objects. The ^nP_r button on the calculator gives the numeric value of a permutation. See also **combination**.

> **Q** Find the permutations of *A*, *B* and *C*; taken two at a time.
> **A** The permutations of *A*, *B* and *C*; taken two at a time are
> AB, AC, BC, BA, CA, CB.
> This is $^3P_2 = 6$ from the calculator.

perpendicular
At right angles to the horizontal.

perpendicular distance   P

perpendicular bisector   See **bisector**.

perpendicular distance   The shortest distance from a point to a line.

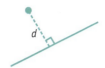

perpendicular lines   Lines that are at right angles to each other. They have **reciprocal** (inverse) gradients (slopes).
For the two gradients, m_1 and m_2; $m_2 = \frac{-1}{m_1}$, $m_1 \neq 0$.
The product of the two gradients equals negative one. $m_1 \times m_2 = -1$.
Also written as $AB \perp CD$.

Q Show that $3x + 2y = 5$ and $2x - 3y = -2$ are perpendicular.
A Find the gradients from the equations:
$3x + 2y = 5$ becomes $y = -\frac{3}{2}x + \frac{5}{2}$ ∴ $m_1 = -\frac{3}{2}$ and
$2x - 3y = -2$ becomes $y = \frac{2}{3}x + \frac{2}{3}$ ∴ $m_2 = \frac{2}{3}$.
Thus $m_1 \times m_2 = -\frac{3}{2} \times \frac{2}{3}$
$= -1$.
Thus the lines are perpendicular.

perspective   A method of drawing objects on a flat surface so that they appear to be three dimensional. Its use was first developed by the Renaissance artists in Italy in the 15th Century.

peta   A prefix meaning one thousand million million times (10^{15}). Symbol P.

Excel Junior High School Maths Study Dictionary

P pH scale

pH scale A scale that measures the acidity or alkalinity of a solution in terms of hydrogen activity. See **logarithmic, scales** also.

pi (π) A constant which is the ratio of the diameter to the circumference of a circle.
$\pi = \frac{C}{d} \approx 3.14$ or $\frac{22}{7}$ or 3.141 592 7 to 7 decimal places.

pico (p) A prefix meaning one-million-millionth (0.000 000 000 001 = 10^{-12}).

pictogram, or picture graph Graphs that use images to represent values.

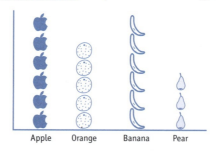

pie graph (or chart) See **sector graph**.

piece work A worker is paid for each item (or piece) produced. A practice usually associated with the garment industry.

pint **Imperial** measure of capacity. Approximately 568 mL.

place holder A symbol which holds the place for an unknown value. This is most usually either □ or a pronumeral such as x. **Zero** is a place holder when using place value.
3400 indicates the number consists of 3 thousands, 4 hundreds, 0 tens and 0 units. Thus the two 0s are place holders to give the correct value for the 3 and the 4.

place value The value a digit has due to its position in a number written in the **Hindu-Arabic** system. See **expanded notation**.

> **Q** Give the value of the 7 and the 4 in 2735.64.
> **A** Place value tells us the 7 is 700 and the 4 is 4 hundredths.

plane A flat surface. Being two-dimensional (2D), it has length and width only.

plane of symmetry The plane that divides a solid into two parts that are mirror images of each other. See also **symmetry**.

plane shape Something that is flat, able to be drawn exactly on paper. Plain shapes lie in one plane and have area but not volume. They are two-dimensional (2D).

plane surface See **plane shape**, above.

platonic solids The set of 5 solids that each has the same regular plane shape as all faces. Three are made with equilateral triangles (tetrahedron, octahedron and icosahedron), one with squares (cube or hexahedron) and one with pentagons (dodecahedron). See also these entries:

tetrahedron (4 sides) octahedron (8) icosahedron (20) cube (6) dodecahedron (12).

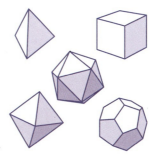

P plotting points

plotting points The process of using a set of coordinate axes to place points to represent a value for each axis. See graphing, on the number plane.

plumb At right angles. A plumb bob is a weight on a string (called a line) that due to gravity indicates the vertical or plumb line. See also spirit level.

plus (+) The name of the symbol for addition.
6 + 7 = 13 is read as six plus seven equals thirteen.

pm See post meridiem.

point
1 Basic element in geometry. Marks a position but has no dimensions.
2 Name given to the decimal point in description.
   17.3 is read as seventeen point three.

point of contact A point at which two geometric figures touch but do not intersect.
A tangent to a circle has a point of contact.

point of intersection Where two graphs meet. Especially applies to straight lines.

Excel Junior High School Maths Study Dictionary

point symmetry

point symmetry When a plane shape repeats itself after half a turn about a point. A rectangle has point symmetry. See also **rotational symmetry**.

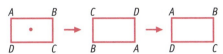

points

on the number line: Points or values can be plotted on the number line to represent a solution or a set of values.

Q Show the set $\{x : x \geq 2\}$ on the number line.
A

on the number plane: Position on the number plane is represented by a point and indicated by **coordinates** (or a number pair). See also **cartesian coordinates**.

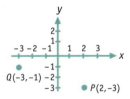

The points $P(2, -3)$ and $Q(-3, -1)$ are shown.

polygon A plane shape with many (poly) sides. The general name for any plane shape or gon. See **pentagon**, **hexagon**, **heptagon**, **octagon**, **nonagon** and **decagon**.

Pentagon   Hexagon   Heptagon   Octagon   Nonagon

polygon, angle sum See **angle sum, of polygon**.

continued over

polygon

polygon, cumulative frequency: See cumulative frequency polygon.
frequency: See frequency polygon.

polyhedron A three-dimensional (3D) figure (solid) whose faces are plane shapes with straight sides (polygons). Pyramids, prisms and the platonic solids are examples. The plural is polyhedra. Polyhedra are divided into prisms, pyramids and others.

polynomial An algebraic expression consisting of two or more terms of only one variable raised to different integral powers.
$P(x) = x^4 - 5x^3 + 6x^2 - 3x + 8$ *is an example of a polynomial.*

polynomial
division of: See division of polynomials.
sketching of: Use the factorisation of a polynomial to find the *x*-intercepts and $P(0)$ to find the *y*-intercept. When a factor is squared the polynomial touches the axis but does not pass through it at that value of *x*. Typical curves can be associated with polynomial order.

Example:
Where $a > 0$.

$y = ax^2 + bx + c$ $y = -ax^2 + bx + c$

$y = ax^3 + bx^2 + cx + d$

$y = ax^4 + bx^3 + cx^2 + dx + e$

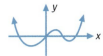

$y = (x - a)(x + b)^2(x - c)$

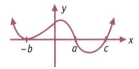

Q Sketch $y = (x - 3)^2(x + 2)(x - 5)$.
A x-intercepts at $x = 3$, -2 and 5. y-intercept at -90.

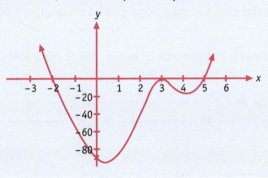

population Used in **statistics**. The total set of persons, things or events under experimentation or investigation. The complete or *universal set*.
census of: See **census**.
sampling a: The people should be selected at random. See *random sample*.

position The location of one object in reference to another. In the number plane, the position of a point is given as **coordinates**.

positive gradient The slope of a line that dips to the left. AB has positive gradient.

P Abscissa

positive numbers (integers) Numbers that are greater than **zero**. Most usually applied to the positive **integers** or positive **directed numbers**. See these entries also.

post meridiem (pm) The label given to times from after noon to midnight. From the Latin meaning of *after midday*.

pound (lb) **Imperial** unit for mass. One pound is equal to 454 grams.

power Another name for **exponent** or **index**. See these entries. Used to read higher indices.

> **Q Give the value of 2^5.**
> **A** $2^5 = 2 \times 2 \times 2 \times 2 \times 2 = 32$ and is read as *2 to the power of 5*.

power set The set of all possible subsets of the given set.
Example: For $\{a, b, c\}$, the power set is $\{\{ \}, \{a\}, \{b\}, \{c\}, \{a, b\}, \{a, c\}, \{b, c\}, \{a, b, c\}\}$. For this 3 element set, the power set has $2^3 = 8$ elements.

predict An instruction to use the information given or that you have just calculated to find an answer.

prediction See **chance (probability)**.

prefix A word before a unit, indicating size. See also **metric system**. Two prefixes are **milli** and **nano**. Examples of their use: millimetre is one thousandth of a metre, while nanosecond is one thousand millionth of a second. This is $\dfrac{1}{1\,000\,000\,000} = 10^{-9}$.

prime factors Factors of a number that are prime. See also **factors**.

> **Q** Give the prime factors of 12.
> **A** 12 has factors of 1, 2, 3, 4, 6, 12. Its prime factors are 2 and 3. $12 = 2^2 \times 3$.

prime meridian The meridian of longitude that passes through Greenwich near London in the United Kingdom. The line from which all other meridians are measured. See also **longitude**.

prime numbers Numbers that have no factors other than themselves and 1. See also **Erasthoneses, sieve of**. Also referred to just as prime. Note: 1 is not considered to be a prime number.
The prime numbers to 100: 2, 3, 5, 7, 11, 13, 17, 19, 23, 29, 31, 37, 41, 43, 47, 53, 59, 61, 67, 71, 73, 79, 83, 89, 97.

principal In finance, money that is either invested or borrowed. Used when calculating interest. See **simple interest** and **compound interest**.

prism A three-dimensional (3D) figure where the cross-section remains the same as the base and the top which is always parallel to the base.

prism
rectangular: See **rectangular prism**.
surface area: See surface area of a solid.
triangular: See **triangular prism**.
volume of: See **volume, of a prism**.

P probability

probability The likelihood of something happening. Conventionally expressed on a scale of zero to one. A rare event has a probability close to zero. A very common event has a probability close to one. An application of relative frequency. See also chance and complementary events.

Probability = $\frac{\text{number of successes}}{\text{total number}}$.

> **Q** Find the probability of drawing a spade from a pack of 52 well-shuffled playing cards.
> **A** The probability is 13 spades divided by 52 cards, or $\frac{32}{52} = \frac{1}{4}$ or 0.25.

probability experiment An activity designed to test a predicted outcome ratio. See also probability, above, chance (probability) and complementary events.

produce To extend an interval such as the side of a plane figure. An instruction. *Produce the side BC to the point D* gives the diagram shown.

product(s) The results from **multiplication**.

> **Q** Find the product of 3, 4 and 5.
> **A** $3 \times 4 \times 5 = 60$.

product of binomials The **multiplication** of two **binomials**. See also these entries. See also perfect square.

> **Q** Expand and simplify: $(3x - 2y)(2x + 5y)$
> **A** $(3x - 2y)(2x + 5y) = 3x(2x + 5y) - 2y(2x + 5y)$
> $= 6x^2 + 15xy - 4xy - 10y^2$
> $= 6x^2 + 11xy - 10y^2$

profit When the **selling price** is more than the **cost price**.
Profit = selling price – cost price.
as a percentage of cost price: Calculated by dividing the profit by the cost price and then multiplying by 100.

> **Q** Calculate the percentage profit when an item is sold for $125 when it cost $95.
> **A** Profit = 125 – 95 = 30. As percentage
> $\frac{30}{95} \times 100 = 31.6\%$ (to 1 decimal place)

progression A sequence of numbers following a given rule. Also called a sequence. There are two main types.
arithmetic progression: A sequence of numbers where each one after the first is found by adding a constant value called the **common difference**.
1, 4, 7, 10, . . .   a common difference of 3. The rule: $T_n = 3n - 2$.
geometric progression. A sequence of numbers where each one after the first is found by multiplying the previous value by a fixed number called the common ratio.
1, 3, 9, 27, . . .   a common ratio of 3.
The rule: $T_n = 3^{(n-1)}$.

progressive taxation A taxation system that changes percentage as income level varies.

Tax rates 2006–07

Taxable income	Tax on this income
$0–$6,000	nil
$6,001–$25,000	15c for each $1 over $6,000
$25,001–$75,000	$2,850 plus 30c for each $1 over $25,000
$75,001–$150,000	$17,850 plus 40c for each $1 over $75,000
over $150,000	$47,850 plus 45c for each $1 over $150,000

pronumerals (variables) Letters used to represent unknown numbers in algebraic expressions and equations. See also **equation** and **expression, algebraic**. $3x + 4 = 13$, uses the pronumeral x to show a relationship.

proper fraction

proper fraction A fraction where the **numerator** is smaller than the **denominator**. Usually just called a fraction. For example $\frac{3}{4}$ is a proper fraction. See also **fraction** and **improper fraction**.

properties of Characteristics of an object.
number: See **number, properties**.
parallelogram: See **parallelogram properties**.
rhombus: See **rhombus properties**.

proportion When the ratios of two sets of two numbers are equal. Thus 4 and 8 are proportional with 12 and 24 as 4:8 = 12:24 = 1:2. Pairs of sides in similar figures are in proportion. A proportion can also be expressed as a fraction equality: $\frac{4}{8} = \frac{12}{24}$.

protractor A measuring instrument used to measure angles.

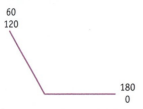
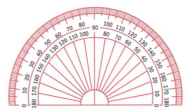

Read the angle measured from the 0 value.
Thus the angle shown is equal to 120°.

prove An instruction in **geometry** and **algebra**. To use a set of formal logical steps to reach a conclusion.
For example the use of the data, aim, construction and proof steps to prove a **theorem** in **geometry**, as shown on the next page.

pyramid

Data: ABC isosceles triangle
Aim: To prove $A\hat{B}C = A\hat{C}B$
Construction: Draw $AD \perp BC$
Proof: In △s ABD, ACD
AB = AC given
AD common
$A\hat{D}B = A\hat{D}C$ construction

∴ △ABD ≡ △ACD (RHS)
∴ $\hat{B} = \hat{C}$
Corresponding angles in congruent triangles.

Pyramid A three-dimensional (3D) shape where the base is a polygon and all other faces are triangles that meet at a point. The bases of the triangles make up the shape that is the base of the pyramid. The pyramid is named by the shape of the base.

Triangular pyramid

Square pyramid

Rectangular pyramid

Pentagonal pyramid

Octagonal pyramid

pyramid, volume of See volume, of pyramid.

P Pythagoras' theorem

Pythagoras' theorem Named after the Greek philosopher and mathematician, 582–500 BC. In a right-angled triangle the square of the hypotenuse is equal to the sum of the squares of the other two sides. This is a very ancient theorem known well before Pythagoras. He was the first to record the result formally.

$$c^2 = a^2 + b^2$$
or
$$AB^2 = CB^2 + AC^2$$

Q Find the value of the pronumerals.

A i $11^2 + 7^2 = a^2$
$\therefore a = \sqrt{170}$

ii $b^2 + 8^2 = 17^2$
$\therefore b = \sqrt{289 - 64}$
$= \sqrt{225}$
$= 15$

Pythagorean triads Sets of three numbers that obey **Pythagoras' theorem**, above.

Examples include 3, 4, 5; 5, 12, 13; 7, 24, 25. Also called a Pythagorean triple.

quadrants The four sections of the number plane. They are numbered in an anti-clockwise direction from the x-axis.

quadrangle A figure with four angles. See **quadrilateral**.

quadratic expression An algebraic **expression** whose highest power is 2. There are no negative or fractional powers. Also called a **quadratic trinomial** when it has three terms.
Example: $x^2 + 5x - 6$ is a quadratic trinomial.

quadratic equation An equation of the general form $ax^2 + bx + c = 0$, where a, b and c are constants and $a \neq 0$.

quadratic equation, solving See also **factorisation**.
by completion of squares: See **completing the square**.
by factors: There are several algorithms used to factorise a quadratic.
cross method: See entry for **cross method**.
splitting the middle term: This method enables the finding of common factors.

$2x^2 - x - 3 = 0$
$2x^2 - 3x + 2x - 3 = 0$
$x(2x - 3) + 1(2x - 3) = 0$
$(2x - 3)(x + 1) = 0$
$\therefore x = 1\frac{1}{2}$ or $x = -1$

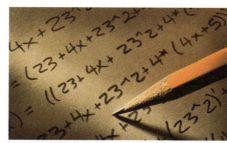

continued over with question and answer example

quadratic formula

Q Solve the following:
i $(x + 2)(x - 2) = 0$
ii $(3x - 2)(3x + 4) = 0$
iii $x^2 - 6x + 8 = 0$
iv $4(x + 2)^2 - 16 = 0$

A i $(x + 2)(x - 2) = 0 \therefore x + 2 = 0$ or $x - 2 = 0$. This gives $x = -2$ or $x = 2$.
ii $(3x - 2)(3x + 4) = 0 \therefore 3x - 2 = 0$ or $3x + 4 = 0$.
This gives $x = \frac{2}{3}$ or $x = -\frac{4}{3} = -1\frac{1}{3}$.
iii $x^2 - 6x + 8 = 0 \therefore (x - 4)(x - 2) = 0$.
This gives $x - 4 = 0$ or $x - 2 = 0$.
Thus $x = 4$ or $x = 2$.
iv $4(x + 2)^2 - 16 = 0 \therefore (x + 2)^2 = 4$.
Then take the square root of both sides. This gives:
$x + 2 = 2$ or $x + 2 = -2$.
Thus $x = 0$ or $x = -4$.

quadratic formula For the general form of the quadratic equation $ax^2 + bx + c = 0$, $a \neq 0$, solutions can be found using the formula:
$$x = \frac{-b \pm \sqrt{b^2 - 4ac}}{2a}$$
There is always a solution as long as the square root can be taken.
This means $b^2 - 4ac \geq 0$. This value is the *discriminant*.

Q Solve $3x^2 - 7x + 3 = 0$ as an exact answer.
A $3x^2 - 7x + 3 = 0$ gives
$$x = \frac{-b \pm \sqrt{b^2 - 4ac}}{2a}$$
$$= \frac{-(-7) + \sqrt{(-7)^2 - 4 \times 3 \times 3}}{2 \times 3}$$
$$= \frac{7 \pm \sqrt{49 - 36}}{6}$$
Thus $x = \frac{7 + \sqrt{13}}{6}$ or $x = \frac{7 - \sqrt{13}}{6}$.

quadratic graphs See **polynomials**.

quadratic trinomial A quadratic expression with three terms. Written in general terms as $ax^2 + bx + c = 0$, $a \neq 0$, $b \neq 0$, $c \neq 0$.

quadrilateral A plane four-sided figure. See separate entries for **diamond**, **kite**, **parallelogram**, **rectangle**, **rhombus**, **square** and **trapezium**.

quadrillion 1 million million million million (10^{24}, British usage) or one thousand thousand thousand million (one thousand million million, 10^{15}, American usage).

quadruple To increase the amount four times.

> **Q** If Joshua invested $500 and quadrupled his money, how much did he now have?
> **A** To quadruple is to multiply by 4. Thus he now has $500 \times 4 = \$2000$.

qualitative data Data that is sorted according to a category (or feature). It is non-numerical. There are two types:
nominal: Sub-groups are needed.
Examples: Gender: boy, girl; or animal: cat, dog, etc.
ordinal: Ranking is needed.
Example: Levels: very high, high, satisfactory, etc.

quantitative data Data in numerical form. That is data which uses numbers to show *how much*, such as height or how many in the family. There are two types, discrete and continuous data.
discrete: *Counted* in exact values. Usually, but not always, whole numbers.
Examples: Goals scored in a game, shoe size.

continued over

Q qualitative data

qualitative data, continuous: *Measured* in a continuous decimal scale.
Examples: mass, temperature, length etc.
See also **continuous data** (e.g. height) and **discrete data** (age in years).

Q Classify the following data using two of the following terms: qualitative, quantitative, nominal, ordinal, discrete and continuous.
  i The number of students present in class.
  ii The vehicle types using a highway.
  iii The hamburger types purchased at a restaurant.
  iv The air temperatures last Monday.

A i Quantitative, discrete.
  ii Qualitative, nominal.
  iii Qualitative, ordinal.
  iv Quantitative, continuous.

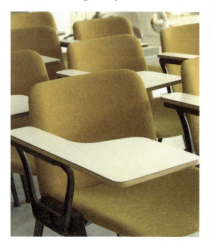

quantity Any property of a quantity whose size can be expressed as a number Usually refers to measurement of length, area, volume, capacity, time, etc.

quart **Imperial** unit of capacity. Equal to two pints. See **pint**. Literally a quarter **gallon**. See this entry also.

quarter One part of four equal parts. See also **fraction**.

230 *Excel Junior High School Maths Study Dictionary*

quarterly An event that occurs four times per year. Often a payment or charge associated with preparing a **budget**.
The water rates are charged four times a year, that is quarterly.

quartile The values that divide a distribution into four equal parts. The first quartile is at the 25% mark, the median is at the 50% mark and the third quartile is at the 75% mark. See also **interquartile range** and **percentile**.

questionnaire A method of **data** collection. Collection done by using mail or similar contact (internet or email). Questions need to be carefully prepared and a range of responses provided (good, poor, bad). A questionnaire can form the basis of an interview or can be left for completion and return. See also **interview**.

quotient The result of a division or to carry out a division.
Find the quotient of …

$$\text{divisor} \overline{)\text{dividend}} \;\; \overset{\text{quotient}}{} + \text{remainder}$$

R radical (sign)

radical (sign) Another name for **root**. See this entry. Also the name for the various signs $\sqrt{}$ $\sqrt[3]{}$ $\sqrt[5]{}$ etc.

radicand The **surd** part of the number that is under the radical or root sign. For $5\sqrt{7}$, the radicand is 7.

radius The distance from the centre of the circle to the circumference. The plural is radii.

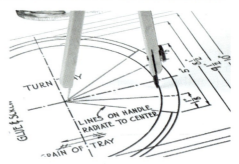

raise An instruction to multiply a number by itself a number of times. See **index** and **power**.

> **Q Raise 3 to the power 4.**
> **A** This means $3 \times 3 \times 3 \times 3 = 3^4$
> $= 81$.

radian An angle measure where the length of arc subtended by the angle equals the radius of the circle containing the angle.

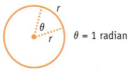

$\theta = 1$ radian

random Not following a pattern or rule. Not able to be predicted. A method of selection designed to ensure that each outcome is equally likely to be chosen.

random numbers

random numbers A set of numbers between 0 and 1 that have been created using a random number generator such as a calculator or computer. Use the RAN() button on a scientific calculator or the rand choice on a graphics calculator.

Random numbers	
02 38 10 98	54 67 58 45
12 58 76 94	54 99 04 68
63 94 46 64	99 96 95 01
23 43 52 56	67 93 13 98
11 03 37 85	88 74 14 91
10 44 56 43	94 50 26 94
63 94 46 64	99 96 95 01
23 43 52 56	67 93 13 98
11 03 37 85	88 74 14 91
52 07 64 48	02 34 25 58

random sample A sample taken so that each member of the population has the same chance of being selected.

random selection See **random sample**, above.

random variable An alternative name for **independent variable**. See this entry.

range **1** Used in statistics. It is the difference between the highest and lowest scores: A measure of **dispersion**.

> **Q** Find the range of the data 3, 5, 8, 11, 13, 17, 23.
> **A** The range is 23 − 3 = 20.

2 The subset of the **co-domain** that consists of the elements selected as the **dependent variable** in a function or relation. See these entries also.

Excel Junior High School Maths Study Dictionary

R rank

rank To place in order either increasing or decreasing.

Q Rank 3, 6, 1, 7, 4, 9, 2 in increasing order.
A This gives: 1, 2, 3, 4, 6, 7, 9.

rate A comparison of unlike quantities written in a definite order. Note: Units are used in this comparison. See **ratio** by contrast. Rates can be expressed as **travel graphs** or as **conversion graphs**.
A V8 Supercar on Conrod Straight will exceed 250 km/h.

rate of interest The percentage at which interest is charged or paid. See **simple interest**.

rates Charges made for services provided by municipal councils and for water.

ratio A comparison of like quantities or numbers written in order. The values in a ratio are whole numbers. The ratio symbol is :. It can also be written as a **fraction**. See also **rational number**. Note: No units are used.

Q Find the ratio of $2.50 to $10.
A Change the values to the same measure: cents. Then the ratio is 250:1000 = 1:4 after simplification of the fraction.

comparing ratios: To compare ratios, compare the fractions.

Q Compare the ratios 3:4 and 2:3.
A $\frac{3}{4} = \frac{9}{12}$ and $\frac{2}{3} = \frac{8}{12}$. Thus the ratio 3:4 > 2:3.

continued over

decreasing in a ratio. To find a new quantity that satisfies the given ratio.

> **Q** Decrease $400 in the ratio of 2:3.
> **A** $\frac{2}{3} \times 400 = 266.\dot{6}$. Thus the value is $266.67.

dividing a quantity: The process to separate the quantity into parts that match the given ratio; by first dividing by the total of the number of parts and then multiplying by the particular ratio.

> **Q** Divide $15 in the ratio of 3:2.
> **A** $3 + 2 = 5$, thus $15 \div 5 = 3$.
> ∴ The two parts are $3 \times 3 = \$9$ and $3 \times 2 = \$6$

increasing in a ratio. To find a new quantity that satisfies the given ratio.

> **Q** Increase $500 in the ratio of 5:3.
> **A** $\frac{5}{3} \times 500 = 833.\dot{3}$. Thus the value is $833.33.

in similar triangles: See **similar triangles**.
trigonometric: Also referred to as ratios of sides of right-angled triangles. See **trigonometric ratios** in separate entries for **cosine ratio**, **sine ratio** and **tangent ratio**.

rational number A number of the form $\frac{a}{b}$, where a and b are integers and $b \neq 0$. A fraction. A member of the infinite set of numbers. See also **improper fraction**.

rationalise To express the denominator in a **surd** fraction as a rational number. Multiply by the conjugate surd.
$$\frac{1}{\sqrt{a} + \sqrt{b}} \times \frac{\sqrt{a} - \sqrt{b}}{\sqrt{a} - \sqrt{b}} = \frac{\sqrt{a} - \sqrt{b}}{a - b}.$$

raw data Data that has been collected but not organised or analysed in any way. See **frequency**, **measures of central tendency** and **dispersion (measures of)** as well as **data**.

R ray

ray A line that has a definite starting point but no end.

real numbers Numbers which are either **rational** or **irrational**. See these entries.

Q Show $-3 \leq x < 2$ on the number line.

A Closed circle indicates $\leq$ Open circle indicates $<$

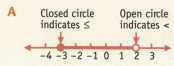

reciprocal The inverse for **multiplication**. The product of a number and its reciprocal is 1. The reciprocal of 3 is $\frac{1}{3}$ and the reciprocal of $\frac{3}{4}$ is $\frac{4}{3}$.

reciprocal relationships These are of the form $xy = k$ where x and y are variables and k is a constant. See **hyperbola**, **coordinates, rectangular (Cartesian)** and the **number plane**.

rectangle A quadrilateral with opposite sides equal and containing a right angle. Alternatively: A **parallelogram** containing a right angle.

Rectangle
area of: See **area, of rectangle**.
golden: See **golden rectangle (mean or section)**.
perimeter of: See **perimeter**.

rectangular numbers R

properties of rectangles:

Opposite sides parallel.   All angles 90°.   Diagonals equal.

Diagonals bisect.   Two axes of symmetry.

 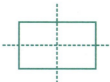

rectangular numbers Natural numbers that can be represented by dots arranged in a rectangle. Thus any natural number that is not a **prime number**.

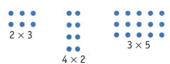

rectangular prism A **prism** where the base is a rectangle. The cross-section is also a rectangle.

rectangular prism, volume of See volume, of a prism.

rectangular pyramid A **pyramid** where the base is a rectangle. The cross-sections are also rectangles that are similar to each other.

rectangular pyramid, volume of See volume, of a pyramid.

R rectilinear

rectilinear Formed from or characterised by straight lines. Thus a triangle is rectilinear while a circle is not.
Note: Rectilinear motion is moving in a straight line.

recurring decimals A decimal where a group of digits repeat.
$\frac{2}{7} = 0.285\,714\,285\,714\,28\ldots = 0.\overline{285714}$ (a line is drawn above the digits that repeat)

recursion Carrying out the current step of a calculation using the result of the previous calculation.
Example: 3, 6, 12, 24, . . . is an example of recursion: double the previous number.

reduce An instruction: To simplify a fraction in its lowest form.

Q Reduce $\frac{9}{12}$ to its lowest form.
A This gives $\frac{3}{4}$ after dividing numerator and denominator by 3.

reducible rate (of interest) Used in association with finance and especially loan calculations. The interest is calculated on the current value of the loan after payments have been made. The determination of the interest at any time is still a simple interest calculation. See also flat rate (of interest).

reduction A smaller version of the original. It is the transformation of a figure so that it has a similar shape. See also dilation and enlargement.

reduction factor See enlargement and dilation.

re-entrant polygon A **polygon** that is not **convex**. Two or more sides slope into the polygon. Also called a **concave** polygon.

reflection The creation of a mirror image. See **axis of symmetry**. Size and shape are retained while orientation is reversed. One of the **transformations**. See this entry also.

reflex angle An angle greater than 180° and less than 360°.

regions

number plane: Areas defined by **inequations**. These may be linear or non-linear in form. The region is most easily found by the substitution of the **coordinates** of a point to see if it is in or out of the region.

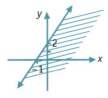

Venn diagrams: See separate entry, **Venn diagram**.

R regression lines

regression lines Lines fitted to bivariate data to help describe a trend. The line shown is a two mean regression line. See also data, bivariate.

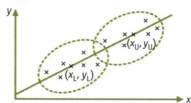

regular A description that applies to plane shapes and solids. The sides and angles of plane figures are equal while the faces of solids are congruent. See also congruence.

Regular hexagon   Cube

relation A connection, correspondence or contrast between a pair of measures, numbers, or objects, etc. A correspondence (map) between the elements of two sets. Also called a relationship. Can be a set of ordered pairs (coordinate) (x, y), a map (arrow diagram, like the one shown) or a graph.

Examples: Fred is taller than Maggie.
$4 > 2$, $y = 2x + 3$ $y \leq 3x - 2$

relative address An address that relates to the cell the formula is in when dealing with a spreadsheet computer program.

relative frequency The fraction made by the frequency of one score over the total of the frequencies. See also experimental probability.

For the data

x	1	2	3	4	5
f	3	6	8	7	2

$\Sigma f = 26$

the relative frequency of 3 is $\frac{8}{26} = \frac{4}{13}$

remainder The value less than the **divisor** that is left when **division** is complete.

$$\text{divisor} \overline{)\text{dividend}} + \text{remainder} \quad\quad 17 \div 5 = 5 \times 3 + 2$$
(quotient above dividend)

repeating decimal A decimal where one digit repeats. See also **recurring decimal**.
$\frac{1}{3} = 0.3333333\ldots = 0.\dot{3}$

representative sample A subset of the whole **population** selected according to criteria that ensures the sample represents the distribution of the elements in the population. See also sample, random **sample**, **sample space** and **statistics**.

respectively Used with lists to relate members of the first list with the corresponding members of the second list.
The points *A, B* and *C* have coordinates (3, 2), (–1, 4) and (5, –3) respectively, means that *A* is the point (3, 2) and so on.

retail price See **selling price**.

reverse The opposite way or the other way around. See also **reflection**.
The reverse of 259 is 952.

revolution A rotation through one complete turn. Equal to 360°. See also **perigon**.

rhombic Referring to a **rhombus**. Thus a rhombic pyramid or rhombic prism have a rhombus as a base.

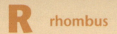 rhombus

rhombus A quadrilateral with all four sides equal. Sometimes referred to as a diamond. Note: A baseball or softball diamond is actually a square.

Rhombus

Softball diamond (which is actually a square)

properties:
Opposite sides parallel:

Opposite angles equal:

Diagonals bisect at right angles:

Two axes of symmetry:

Richter scale The logarithmic scale used to measure earth movements. The index is the value quoted. Thus an earthquake of 2 is ten times stronger than an earthquake of 1 and so on. Named after Charles F Richter, 1900-1985, US seismologist.

right (solids) Short for upright. Means at right angles to the base.

Right cone

Right cylinder

Right prism

right angle An angle of 90°. See also **perpendicular**. Shown by the symbol ∟ or ⊥.

right-angled The adjective. Containing or defined by a right angle.

Right-angled triangle

Right-angled triangular pyramid

Rigid A shape that can not be deformed. A triangle is the basis of all rigid shapes.

Roman numerals Letter symbols used to express numbers. Larger values are written first.

To express 1, 2 or 3 the symbol is repeated. 4 is 1 less than 5. Note: There is only one value subtraction. Thus 4 is IV not IIII and 9 is IX not VIIII and so on.

1 is I	3 is III	4 is IV	5 is V	8 is VIII
9 is IX	10 is X			
40 is IL	50 is L	80 is LXXX	90 is XC	100 is C
400 is CD	500 is D	800 is DCCC	900 is CM	1000 is M

Larger numbers are shown with a bar above the symbol. This indicates 1000 times the original value. Thus $\bar{V}$ is 5000, $\bar{L}$ is 50 000 and so on.

root Common usage for **square root**. See this entry. See also **cube root**.

R rotation

rotation To turn an object through a given angle about a fixed point. Shape and size are retained. One of the **transformations**. See this entry also.

rotational symmetry A shape can be spun about a point so that it repeats its shape more than once in a rotation. See also **point symmetry** and **symmetry**.

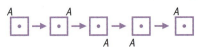

Square: Rotational symmetry of order 4.

round(ing) To make an approximation to a set standard (number of decimal places, nearest hundred, etc). See also **significant figures**.

to the nearest multiple of 10: Consider the digit in the position after and then apply the rule that 5 or more is rounded up, while less than 5 remains unchanged.

> **Q1 Round 77 to the nearest 10.**
> **A** 77 is 80, (nearest ten).
>
> **Q2 Round 247 to the nearest 100.**
> **A** 247 is 200, (nearest hundred).

to a number of decimal places (dp): Consider the digit in the position after and then apply the rule that 5 or more is rounded up.

> **Q1 Round 0.64 to one decimal place.**
> **A** The 4 after the 6 is < 5, thus do not round up: 0.64 is 0.6 (1dp).
>
> **Q2 Round 2.4738 to 3 decimal places.**
> **A** The 8 after the 3 is > 5, thus round up: 2.4738 is 2.474 (3dp).

route A **path**. It is the trace of a journey from start to finish.

row A horizontal arrangement. See also **column**.

royalty (royalties plural) Earnings from the ownership of a copyright. A musician or an author receives a royalty on the sale of their music or book. It is usually calculated as a **percentage** of the retail price of the work.

> **Q** Joanne the singer receives a royalty of 15% of the price of her CD. If she sells $145\,000$ worth of CDs, what is her royalty?
> **A** Royalty = $145\,000 \times 0.15$
>   = $21\,750$.
> Thus Joanne receives $21\,750.

rule(s) An instruction or instructions to be followed.
Example: For the sequence 3, 6, 12, 24, . . . ; the **rule** is start at 3 and double the number each time.

ruler and compass constructions This means only these instruments are used (certainly no **protractor**). There are usually no angle measurements used in the construction.

S salary

salary Payment for work performed by staff, expressed as an **annual** sum. It is usually paid in fortnightly or monthly instalments. Usually applies to positions where there is an expectation that no overtime will be paid. An example is an executive position in the organisation.

> **Q** Hwang receives $87 500 per annum as his salary. Find his fortnightly payment.
> **A** Payment = $87500 \times \frac{14}{365}$
> = 3356.16.
> Thus Hwang receives $3356.16 per fortnight (to the nearest cent).

same Identical, alike, unchanged, not different.

sample Part (a subset) of a **population**. See **random sample** and also **sample space**, below.

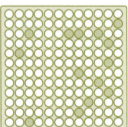

sample size The number of people or objects in the **sample**.

sample space The term used to describe all the possible outcomes when a simple event takes place.

> **Q** Give the sample space for the event; roll a six-sided dice.
> **A** The sample space is 1, 2, 3, 4, 5, 6.

sampling Where a small portion (a **representative sample**) of a **population** is surveyed or examined. If the sample is to reflect the whole population, then a random process is used to ensure an even distribution. In addition the sample must be large enough to give a fair indication of the total population. Can be done with or without replacement. See also **random sample**.

satisfy Refers to a value that makes an **equation** or **inequation** true or correct. $x = 5$ satisfies $3x + 2 = 17$ and also satisfies $3x + 3 > 17$. Thus both the equation and the inequation are true for the value $x = 5$.

scale The **ratio** between the measurement on a map or plan and the equivalent measurement on the ground. Standard Australian survey maps have a scale of 1:10 000, while house plans are often 1 cm: 1 m = 1: 100.

scale drawing A drawing of a plane shape or object drawn to exact measurements, using a **scale**. See above.

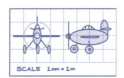
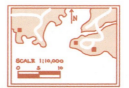

scale factor See **enlargement**.

scalene triangle A triangle where all sides are different lengths and thus the angles are all different values.

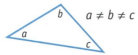

scatter diagram A graph with points plotted to show a relationship between two **quantative variables**, such as height versus mass. Each dot represents an individual case. Also called **scatter plot**.

Positive relationship

Negative relationship

No relationship

scatter plot See **scatter diagram**, above.

scientific notation A number that is written as the **product** of a number from 1 to less than 10 and a power of 10. Also called standard notation or standard form. Used with very large and very small numbers; especially when comparisons are needed.

> **Q** Give 476 593 and 0.000 417 in scientific notation.
> **A** $476\,593 = 4.76593 \times 10^5$ and
> $0.000417 = 4.17 \times 10^{-4}$.

score An amount obtained in a test or a competition. See **statistics**.

secant S

secant A line that intersects a circle in at least two points. See also **tangent**.

second A measurement of:
angle: One sixtieth of a minute. A minute is also one sixtieth of a degree.
60″ = 1′, 60′ = 1°
position: The position between first and third. See **ordinal numbers**.

time: One sixtieth of a minute. A minute is also one sixtieth of an hour.
60 s = 1 min, 60 min = 1 h.
Note: The calculator angle button can be used to enter times for calculation.

section The flat surface revealed when a solid shape is cut through in any direction. See **cross section**.

sector A part of a circle formed by an arc of a circle and two radii drawn from the ends of the arc.

sector
Area of: The fraction of the area of the circle found by multiplying by the angle of the sector in degrees and dividing by 360.

$$A = \frac{80}{360} \times \pi \times 6^2$$
$$= 25.13 \ u^2 \text{ (to 2 decimal places)}$$

continued over

Excel Junior High School Maths Study Dictionary 249

sector graph

perimeter of a sector: The sum of the lengths of the two radii and the length of the arc.

$$P = 5 + 5 + \frac{70}{360} \times 2 \times \pi \times 5$$
$$= 16.1u \text{ (to 1 decimal place)}$$

sector graph A graph drawn on a circle where a sector of the circle represents a percentage of the whole **population** being displayed. Also called a pie chart or pie graph due to its shape and the sectors appear as *pieces of the pie*. See also **bar graph, divided**.

segment of a circle The two parts of a circle cut off by a **chord** or **secant**. The larger is the major segment and the other the minor segment.

selling price For the seller, the price paid when an item is sold. Also called the retail price. For the purchaser this is their cost price. See also **cost price**.

semicircle Half of a circle. When a circle is cut into two equal parts by the **diameter**.

semicircular arc Half the circumference of a circle.

sentence, mathematical A statement in mathematics, such as an equation. See this entry.

sequence A pattern of numbers or objects arranged according to a rule.

○ □ △   ○ □ △   ○

series
arithmetic: The sum of the terms of an arithmetic progression (sequence).
1 + 4 + 7 + 10 + . . . is an example.
geometric: The sum of the terms of a geometric progression (sequence).
1 + 4 + 16 + 64 + . . . is an example.

set A collection of things defined as being members. They are usually defined by listing their elements.
The set of letters of the alphabet is {a, b, c, . . ., x, y, z}

shadow projection The two-dimensional (2D) image projected on a plane surface of a three-dimensional (3D) object illuminated by a light source. An example is a person's shadow on the ground. See also top view, side view and front view.

shaded areas See area, of shaded figures.

shapes See plane shapes and platonic solids.

shift key or 2ndF key The calculator key that enables the other calculator functions to be used. These functions are usually marked in yellow (as shown).

short division

short division Where the remainders are written in the **dividend**.

Q Use short division to find 368 ÷ 7.

A $7\overline{)36^18}$ r4. Thus $358 \div 7 = 52\frac{4}{7}$. Can also be presented as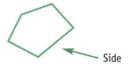

SI system The international system of units (*Système Internationale d'Unités*), the **metric system**. See this entry.

side A line that is part of the perimeter of a **two-dimensional (2D)** shape.

Side

side view The shape of a three-dimensional (3D) object as seen from the side. See also **front view** and **top view**.

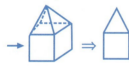 

sieve of Eratosthenes See **Eratosthenes, sieve of**.

Sigma The eighteenth letter of the **Greek alphabet**.
Σ is the summation sign.
σ is the symbol for **standard deviation of a population** in **statistics**.

Sign A symbol used to show an operation or relationship. See separate entries for:

addition	+	multiplication	×
division	÷	order of operations	
indices	x^2	subtraction	−

signed numbers See **directed numbers**.

significant figures (sig fig)

significant figures (sig fig) A form of rounding. See also **scientific notation**.
326 had 3 significant figures, 0.00213 also has 3 significant figures (count starts at 2); while 1.004 has 4 significant figures (count starts at 1).

Q1 Give 374 530 correct to 3 significant figures.
A 374 are the first 3 figures counted. Thus 374 530 is rounded to 375 000 (to 3 sig fig).

Q2 Give 374 530 in scientific notation correct to 3 significant figures.
A 374 are the first 3 figures counted. Thus 374 530 is rounded to 375 000 (to 3 sig fig) and this becomes 3.75×10^5.

similar figures Figures that have the same shape but different sizes. Corresponding angles are equal and corresponding sides have the same **ratio**. An exact **enlargement** or **reduction**.

similar triangles Triangles with the same shape and different sizes. The sides are in same **ratio** in matching or corresponding pairs.
See **similar triangle tests**, below.

similar triangle tests Similar triangles are an example of **similar figures**. Triangles are similar if:

1 The sides of one triangle are in a constant ratio with the three corresponding sides of the other triangle.

2 The three angles in one triangle are equal to the corresponding angles in the other triangle.

$$\frac{d}{a} = \frac{e}{b} = \frac{f}{c}$$

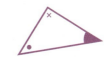

continued over

S similar triangle tests

3 An angle in one triangle is equal to an angle in the other, and the sides about these angles are in **proportion**. See this entry also.

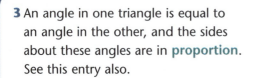

Q1 Find the size of the angle y and give your reasons.

A The triangles are similar as the sides are in the same ratio. Thus $y = 37°$ (corresponding angles equal).

Q2 Find the value of the pronumeral and give your reasons.

 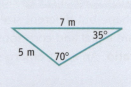

A The triangles are similar as the angles are equal in pairs. Thus a is 3.5 m.

Q3 Find the value of the pronumeral and give your reasoning.

A The ratios about the equal angles are equal $\left(\frac{3}{5} = \frac{6}{10}\right)$ and thus the triangles are similar. Thus $\frac{3}{6} = \frac{6}{x}$ and $x = 12$.

---

simple event An event in which each outcome is equally likely. For example the rolling of a die has the equally likely outcomes: 1, 2, 3, 4, 5, and 6.

simple fraction See **fraction**.

simple interest Interest paid on the original **principal**. The same interest is paid for each time period. The calculation uses the formula $I = PRT$, where P is the principal, R the rate (as a decimal) for the term and T the number of terms. A second formula is $I = \frac{Prt}{100}$, where P is the principal, r the rate (as a percentage) per year (pa) and t the number of years.

> **Q1** Find the simple interest on $760 at 6% pa for 4 years.
> **A** $I = PRT = 760 \times 0.06 \times 4$
> $ = 182.4$. Thus the interest is $182.40.
> or $I = \frac{Prt}{100} = \frac{760 \times 6 \times 4}{100}$
> $\phantom{or I = \frac{Prt}{100}} = 182.4$. Thus the interest is $182.40.
>
> **Q2** Find the simple interest on $12 000 at 8% pa for 30 days.
> **A** The daily rate of interest is $0.08 \div 365 = 0.000219179$ and $T = 30$
> $\therefore I = PRT = 12000 \times 0.0002192 \times 30$
> $ = 78.90$. Thus the interest is $78.90.

simple random sample See **random sample**.

simplest expression An instruction which means to collect all terms and take out any **common factors**. Note: $a(b + c)$ is considered simpler than $ab + ac$, as there is one term rather than two.

> **Q** Give the simplest expression for $3x + 5 + 3x - 2$
> **A** The simplest expression for
> $3x + 5 + 3x - 2 = 6x + 3$

simplest form For a **fraction**. A fraction reduced to a form where the numerator and denominator have no factors in common, other than the number one.
Example: $\frac{6}{12}$ is $\frac{1}{2}$ in simplest form.

simplify 1 To write the given expression in its simplest form by carrying out any possible operations and collecting like terms. See also **simplest expression**, previous page.

2 An instruction which is sometimes incorrectly used when you are asked to find the answer to an equation that needs to be first simplified (as in 1 above), usually by carrying out one or more of the four basic operations ($+, -, \times, \div$). See also **solve**.

simulation The process of studying a complex system by making a mathematical model and then studying that, especially with a computer. The process is significantly useful if the system is difficult to measure or dangerous.

simultaneous equations Equations occurring at the same time. The solution (intersection) found by either **substitution** or **elimination**.

elimination method: The coefficients of one of the variables are made equal by multiplication. One equation is then subtracted from the other, eliminating one of the variables (unknowns). Works only with **linear equations**.

> **Q** Solve simultaneously $2x + 3y = 8$
> $3x - y = 1$
>
> **A** $2x + 3y = 8$
> becomes $6x + 9y = 24$ ($\times 3$)
> $3x - y = 1$
> becomes $6x - 2y = 2$ ($\times 2$)
> This gives $11y = 22$ after subtraction.
> The result $y = 2$ follows.
> Substituting $y = 2$ into the second equation gives $3x - 2 = 1$
> The result $x = 1$ follows.

graphically: The two graphs are drawn and the intersection(s) are read from the graph.

> **Q** Solve $y = 2x + 3$ and $y = 5 - 3x$ graphically.
> **A** From the graph the approximate intersection point is (0.4, 3.8).

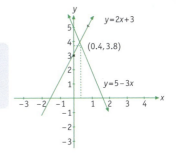

substitution method: The expression of one variable in terms of the other is substituted from the simple equation into the more complex equation (usually the one with higher powers).
$y = 2x + 4$ and $y = x^2 + 3x - 2$ gives
$2x + 4 = x^2 + 3x - 2$
Thus $x^2 + x - 6 = 0 \Rightarrow (x + 3)(x - 2) = 0$
Which gives $x = -3$ or $x = 2$ and then $y = -2$ and $y = 8$
The two intersection points are $(-3, -2)$ and $(2, 8)$.

sine ratio Used in trigonometry in a right-angled triangle. It is found by calculating the value $\dfrac{\text{opposite}}{\text{hypotenuse}}$. It is abbreviated sin.
See also **trigonometry, cosine** and **tangent**.

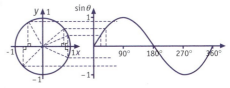

A graph can represent the values of the sine of an angle for angle values from 0° to 360°.

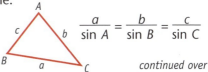

sine rule Used to find sides and angles in non right-angled triangles when given a matching side and angle in the triangle.

$$\frac{a}{\sin A} = \frac{b}{\sin B} = \frac{c}{\sin C}$$

continued over

Q Find the value of the pronumeral.

A As the triangle is non-right-angled and there is a side-angle pair, use the sine rule.

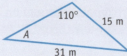

$\dfrac{31}{\sin 110°} = \dfrac{15}{\sin A}$, Thus $31 \sin A = 15 \sin 110°$ and

$\sin A = \dfrac{15 \sin 110°}{31} = 0.4547$. Thus $A = \sin^{-1} 0.4547 = 27°3'$

size The dimension or magnitude of something, usually a **plane shape** or **solid**.

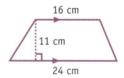

sketch(ing) An instruction to draw something, which while it is neat, is not necessarily totally accurate in its measurements. Often implies a three-dimensional (3D) drawing or a simple graph.

skew lines Lines that do not meet as they are not in the same plane.

AD and BF are skew lines.
DH and AB are also skew lines.

skip counting Counting from a given starting point using multiples of a natural number.
Examples: {2, 4, 6, . . .} and {7, 12, 17, 22, . . .}

slant height The distance from the **vertex** to the base of a right cone or from the vertex of a right pyramid to the base of a triangular face. Usually calculated using **Pythagoras' theorem**.

 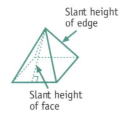 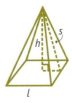

Note: The right pyramid also has the slant height of an edge.

> **Q** Find the slant-height of the cone with radius of 6 cm and height of 15 cm.
>
> **A** $s^2 = r^2 + h^2$ gives $s^2 = 6^2 + 15^2 = 261$
> Thus $s = \sqrt{261} = 16.2$ cm (to 1 decimal place)

slope see **gradient** (*m*).

slope of a line See **gradient formula**.

small circle Any circle on a **sphere** that is not a great circle. The parallels of **latitude** are small circles. See **great circle** also.

snowflake curve The curve produced by dividing each side of an **equilateral triangle** into three equal parts and then constructing an equilateral triangle on the middle third. This process is repeated on each of the new equilateral triangles repeatedly as long as triangles can be drawn. See also **fractal**.

solids Three-dimensional (3D) figures that occupy space. See **nets of solids**, **cone**, **cylinder**, **prism**, **pyramid** and **sphere**.

solution of equation, find the An instruction to find the values of a variable (usually x) that satisfy the equation. To **solve** the equation.

Q1 Find the solution of $x^2 - 4x - 5 = 0$.
A $x^2 - 4x - 5 = 0$ gives $(x + 1)(x - 5) = 0$, and thus $x = -1$, $x = 5$
Q2 Find the solution of $2^x = 8$.
A $2^x = 8 = 2^3$ and thus $x = 3$.

solve An instruction to find the answer; usually involving one of the four basic operations $(+, -, \times, \div)$.

Q Solve $7x + 5 = 19$.
A $7x + 5 = 19$ gives $7x + 5 - 5 = 19 - 5$. Thus $7x = 14$ and $x = 2$.
See also **equations**.

soma cube Formed by joining seven specialised pieces together. These pieces are made from individual cubes.

some A descriptor; meaning not the entire whole, but at least one.
Some of the group remained after the first round of the elimination.

sort To group objects according to set criteria. Often displayed in a **Venn diagram**.

space The three-dimensional (3D) region in which objects exist.

span To stretch from one side to the other.
The Sydney Harbour Bridge is a single span bridge.

spatial Things that are related to, or happening in space.

speed A measurement of distance travelled per unit of time. See also **rate**.
Speed = $\frac{\text{Distance}}{\text{Time}}$.
The speed of all vehicles is restricted to 40 km/h past schools.

sphere

sphere A solid made by rotating a circle on a diameter to make a single surface where every point is a constant distance from the centre. A perfectly round ball. The planets are approximate spheres.

spinner A thin disc or **polygon** used in games and statistical experiments.

spiral A plane curve moving around a fixed point at an ever increasing or decreasing distance from the point.

Fixed point

spirit level Used in building and construction to give a true horizontal or vertical surface. A bubble of air is inside a slightly curved tube containing liquid. The air bubble rises to the curved part of the tube thus showing when it is horizontal. Used in a rectangular container as a spirit level or on a line (string). See also **plumb**.

split-stem (technique) Use with a stem-and-leaf plot to give narrower class intervals. See also **stem-and-leaf plot**.

The stem 1* is used for 10–14
The stem 1 is used for 15–19

Excel Junior High School Maths Study Dictionary

spread, measures of

spread, measures of See **measures of spread**.

spreadsheet A rectangular array of cells, many of which contain information or **equations**. Usually generated by a computer program such as Microsoft Excel. A variety of graphs can be generated from the data in the spreadsheet.

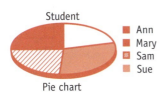
Pie chart

	A	B	C
1	Student	Wages week 1 ($)	Wages week 2 ($)
2	Amy	40	50
3	Mary	60	45
4	Sam	45	60
5	Sue	50	40

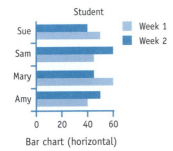
Bar chart (horizontal)

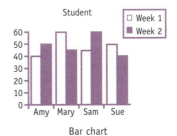
Bar chart

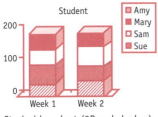
Stacked bar chart (3D and shadow)

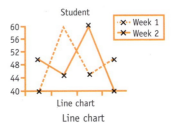
Line chart

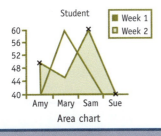
Area chart

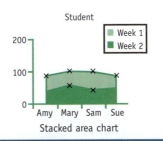
Stacked area chart

Excel Junior High School Maths Study Dictionary

S Square

square A plane shape with four sides all equal and containing a right angle. A quadrilateral. See also right-angle.
area of: See area of, quadrilateral.
magic: See magic square.
properties of:
Opposite sides are parallel.
All angles are right angles.
Diagonals equal.
Diagonals bisect at right angles.
Four axes of symmetry.

square An instruction: To multiply a number by itself.

Q Find the square of 4.
A Square 4 means $4^2 = 4 \times 4$
$ = 16$.

square, perfect See perfect square.

square
centimetre: cm^2. A measure of area. Measures 1 cm by 1 cm.
kilometre: A measure of large areas. 1 km by 1 km. See also hectare.
$1 \ km^2 = 100 \ ha = 1\ 000\ 000 \ m^2$
metre: m^2. The SI standard unit of area measure. Measures 1 m by 1 m.

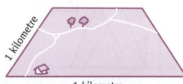

1 kilometre

square number(s)

square number(s) The product obtained when a **natural number** is multiplied by itself. They can also be represented by dots arranged in the shape of squares. Has an odd number of distinct elements in its **factor** set. See also **triangular numbers**.
$1 \times 1 = 1$, $2 \times 2 = 4$, $3 \times 3 = 9$, etc

16 has a factor set {1, 2, 4, 8, 16}: a set of 5 elements.

square root The number that when multiplied by itself gives the original value. The square root may be either rational or irrational. See also **root**.
$\sqrt{9} = 3$ because $3 \times 3 = 9$,   Also $(\sqrt{2})^2 = 2$

squares An **imperial measurement** of area, especially within buildings. A square is 10 feet by 10 feet and is approximately 9.3 m².

squares, difference of See **difference of two squares**.

standard deviation (σ) of a population A measure of spread of **data**. Used to compare the concentration of data about a **mean**. Represented by the 18th Greek letter **sigma**. Given by the formula:
$\sigma = \sqrt{\dfrac{\Sigma(x - \bar{x})^2}{n}}$, where x is the score, n the number of scores and $\bar{x}$, the mean of the scores. Usually found using the statistics mode of a calculator.

Note: There is a separate calculation for the sample standard deviation:
$S_x = \sqrt{\dfrac{\Sigma(x - \bar{x})^2}{n - 1}}$.

standard (index) form See **scientific notation**.

standard notation See **scientific notation**.

standard pack of cards 52 playing cards of two colours (red and black) with 4 suits (hearts, clubs, spades and diamonds). There are 13 cards in each suit {2, 3, 4, 5, 6, 7, 8, 9, 10, Jack, Queen, King, Ace}.

standard unit of measurement See **SI system** and **metric system**.

start The beginning. See also **route**.

state An instruction: To give the correct answer. Another way of saying find.

statistics The interpretation of **data** through the use of **measures of central tendency** and **measures of spread**. See these entries.

stem The first numeral in a **stem-and-leaf plot table**, below. See also **split-stem technique**.

stem-and-leaf plot (table) A method of displaying the distribution of a set of data. Also known as a **stem plot**.
The data 20, 25, 26, 27, 28, 33, 36, 39, 39, 43, 44, 44, 47, 48 appears as:

```
2 | 0 5 6 7 8
3 | 3 6 9 9
4 | 3 4 4 7 8
```

step graph A graph made up of several horizontal intervals or steps. The end of one horizontal line and the start of the next are vertically aligned. Each line has an open circle at one end and a closed circle at the other. The graph is **discontinuous** due to the gaps. Often used to show rates or costs that jump from one value to another (such as postal rates or parking rates).

straight angle An angle of 180°. Equal to half of a **revolution** or two right-angles.

straight line The shortest distance between two points.

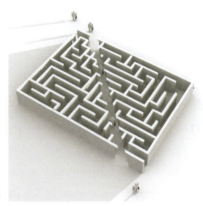

straight line graphs See **line graphs**.

straight line equation See **equation of straight line**.

stratified random sampling Used where there are a number of separate subgroups in a **population** that need to be recognised in the analysis of **data**. Random sampling is done on each subgroup to ensure that the population is fairly represented. See also **random sample**.
If a population was made up of men, women and children then random samples would need to be taken of each group in proportion to the relative numbers of each group.

subject

change of: An instruction that means to make another **variable** the subject. The process involves **reverse** operations.

> **Q** Change the subject of $v = u + at$ to t.
> **A** Thus $v = u + at \Leftrightarrow v - u = at \Leftrightarrow t = \frac{v-u}{a}$.

of an equation: To isolate the **pronumeral (variable)** named, by itself, on the left-hand side of the equation. *Change the subject of the equation to …*

of a formula: the pronumeral or variable that is separate from the others. *For example in the formula $I = PRT$, I is the subject.*

subset

A set within a set. A part of a set. The odd numbers $\{1, 3, 5, 7, ...\}$ are a subset of the counting numbers $\{1, 2, 3, 4, 5, 6, 7, ...\}$.

substitution

The replacement of a **variable** in an equation or formula. Used to ensure that the value is correct (**equation**) or to obtain a value (**formula**).

> **Q1** Check that $(3, 1)$ satisfies $y = 4 - x$.
> **A** $y = 4 - x$ becomes $y = 4 - 3 = 1$ which equals y.
> **Q2** For $r = 3$, find V when $V = \frac{4}{3}\pi r^3$.
> **A** $V = \frac{4}{3}\pi r^3 = \frac{4}{3}\pi \times 3^3 = 113.1$ (to 1 decimal place).

substitution method for simultaneous equations

See **simultaneous equations, substitution method**.

subtract

An instruction, meaning to take away. See also **difference** and **subtraction (−)**.

subtraction (−)

Finding the difference between two numbers by taking the smaller from the larger. The opposite to addition. See also separate entries for **directed numbers**, **fractions**, **integers**, **mixed numbers**, and **whole numbers**.

subtraction (−)

subtraction, of decimals: Place the decimal points under each other. Include zero(s) to fill gaps.

> **Q** Subtract 3.71 from 4.2.
> **A** Use the vertical algorithm
> $$\begin{array}{r} 4.20 \\ -\ 3.71 \\ \hline 0.49 \end{array}$$ including the 0.

of directed numbers: Obey the rule of signs.

> **Q1** Find $-2 - 3$
> **A** $-2 - 3 = -5$

Subtracting a negative number is the same as adding a positive number.

> **Q2** Find $-3 - -4$
> **A** $-3 - -4$ becomes $-3 + 4 = +1$

of fractions: First express each separate fraction with the same (lowest common) **denominator** and then subtract the resultant **numerators**.

> **Q** Find $\frac{3}{4} - \frac{2}{3}$
> **A** $\frac{3}{4} - \frac{2}{3} = \frac{3 \times 3 - 4 \times 2}{12}$
> $= \frac{9 - 8}{12}$
> $= \frac{1}{12}.$

of fractions in algebra: Use the same process as for fractions.

> **Q** Find $\frac{3a}{4} - \frac{2a}{3}$
> **A** $\frac{3a}{4} - \frac{2a}{3} = \frac{3a \times 3 - 2a \times 4}{12}$
> $= \frac{9a - 8a}{12}$
> $= \frac{a}{12}.$ ($1a$ is written as a).

Note: The result is left as an **improper fraction**.

continued over

S subtraction methods

subtraction, of mixed numbers: Subtract the whole numbers and then subtract the fractions.

Q Find $2\frac{1}{3} - 1\frac{2}{5}$.

A $2\frac{1}{3} - 1\frac{2}{5} = 2 - 1 + \frac{1}{3} - \frac{2}{5}$

$= 1 + \frac{5-6}{15}$

$= 1 - \frac{1}{15}$

$= \frac{14}{15}$

or $2\frac{1}{3} - 1\frac{2}{5} = 1\frac{1}{3} - \frac{2}{5}$

$= \frac{4}{3} - \frac{2}{5}$

$= \frac{20 - 6}{15}$

$= \frac{14}{15}$

of surds: Surds can only be subtracted if they are the same type.

Q Find $3\sqrt{3} - 2\sqrt{3} - \sqrt{5}$.

A Only $\sqrt{3}$s can be simplified. Thus $3\sqrt{3} - 2\sqrt{3} - \sqrt{5} = \sqrt{3} - \sqrt{5}$.

of whole numbers:

Q Subtract 34 from 47.

A Use the vertical algorithm.
```
  47
- 34
  13
```

subtraction methods Two **algorithms** are available.

decomposition: The next highest place value is broken down to allow the subtraction to take place.

Q 53 − 17

A The 50 is decomposed into 40 + 10 which transforms the 3 into 13.

$$\begin{array}{r} {}^{4}\cancel{5}{}^{1}3 \\ -\ 17 \\ \hline 36 \end{array}$$

subtrahend

equal additions: An equal amount is added to both the **subtrahend** and the **minuend** to allow the subtraction to occur. Also known as borrow and pay back method.

Q 53 – 17
A 10 is added to the 3 to make 13 and to allow the question to remain unchanged 10 is added to the 17 to make 27.

$$\begin{array}{r} \overset{1}{5}\overset{}{3} \\ -\overset{2}{\cancel{1}}7 \\ \hline 36 \end{array}$$

subtrahend The number that is to be subtracted from another number.

63 – 17 = 46

minuend – **subtrahend** = result (or difference)

subtend If the ends of an interval AB are joined to a point C the angle formed ($A\hat{C}B$) is said to be the angle subtended at C by AB. When A and B are on a circle then the angle at C is subtended by the arc AB or the chord AB. The arc AB can also subtend an angle at the centre O.

successive discounts A **discount** on an already discounted price.

Q Find the final price when a drill costing $130 is sold at a 15% off sale when a further builder's discount of 12% applies.
A $130 \times 0.85 = 110.5$ gives the first discount and $110.50 \times 0.88 = 97.24$ the second. The final price is $97.24.

sum The total using addition. See also **addition**.

Q Find the sum of 7 and 8.
A $7 + 8 = 15$

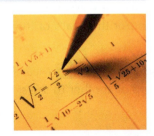

of an arithmetic sequence: Given by the formulas
$S_n = \frac{n}{2}[2a + (n-1)d]$ and $S_n = \frac{n}{2}(a + l)$

continued over

of a geometric sequence: Given by the formula $S_n = \dfrac{a(1-r^n)}{1-r} = \dfrac{a(r^n-1)}{r-1}$, $r \neq 1$.

of an infinite geometric sequence: Given by the formula $S_L = \dfrac{a}{1-r}$, where $|r| < 1$. Known as the limiting sum or sum to **infinity**.

of two cubes: See **cubes, sum of two**.

sum, of two polynomials: Add only the like terms.

> **Q** Find $P(x) + Q(x)$, where
> $P(x) = 3x^4 - 7x^3 + 8x - 4$ and
> $Q(x) = x^3 + 5x^2 - 7x - 3$.
> **A** $P(x) + Q(x)$
> $= 3x^4 - 7x^3 + 8x - 4 + (x^3 + 5x^2 - 7x - 3)$.
> $= 3x^4 - 7x^3 + 8x - 4 + x^3 + 5x^2 - 7x - 3$
> $= 3x^4 - 6x^3 + 5x^2 + x - 7$

summary statistics Measures such as **mean**, **median** and **mode**. See these entries.

superannuation A form of insurance or investment where employer or employer and employee both contribute. There is a fixed percentage of income that the employer must contribute as legislated by the Federal Government. Where the employee also contributes, a **percentage** of the employee's  **salary** or **wage** is deducted. Allows for the payment of a pension on retirement and/or the death of the contributor.

superimpose Means to place one figure or object on top of another to see similarities and differences.

supplement

supplement In an instruction: The second of two angles that add to 180 degrees.

> **Q** Find the supplement of 120°.
> **A** 180 − 120 = 60.
> Thus the supplement of 120° is 60°.

supplementary angles Two angles that add to 180°. See also **parallel lines** and **cointerior angles**.

119° 61°

surd An alternative name for some **irrational numbers**. See this entry and also **rationalise**. $\sqrt{3}$ is a surd while = $\sqrt{4}$ = 2 is not.
Note: Some irrational numbers such as π are **transcendental numbers**.
simplifying: See **surd operations**, below.
conjugate: The surd expression which when multiplied by the original surd gives a value without surds. Used in rationalisation of surds and relies on the **difference of two squares**.

> **Q** Give the conjugate surd for $2\sqrt{5} - \sqrt{3}$
> **A** The conjugate is $2\sqrt{5} + \sqrt{3}$ as $(2\sqrt{5} - \sqrt{3})(2\sqrt{5} + \sqrt{3}) = (2\sqrt{5})^2 - (\sqrt{3})^2$
> $= 20 - 3$
> $= 17$

entire: To reverse the process of **simplification**.

> **Q** Express $5\sqrt{3}$ as an entire surd.
> **A** $5\sqrt{3} = \sqrt{25} \times \sqrt{3}$
> $= \sqrt{25 \times 3}$
> $= \sqrt{75}$

quadratic: A surd of the form $\sqrt{2}$ or $\frac{5 + \sqrt{3}}{4}$. An older form of reference for a type of **irrational number**.

surd form The expressing of an **index** (or exponent) as an **irrational number**. *The surd form of $a^{\frac{1}{x}}$ is $\sqrt[x]{a}$.*

surd operations

surd operations

addition: Only like surds can be added.

Q Simplify $\sqrt{3} + 2\sqrt{3} - \sqrt{27}$.
A $\sqrt{3} + 2\sqrt{3} - \sqrt{27} = \sqrt{3} + 2\sqrt{3} - 3\sqrt{3}$
$= 0$.

division: The division of two surds is the surd of the division.

Q Find $\sqrt{12} \div \sqrt{3}$.
A $\sqrt{12} \div \sqrt{3} = \sqrt{12 \div 3}$
$= \sqrt{4}$
$= 2$

multiplication: The product of two surds is the surd of the product.

Q Find $\sqrt{12} \times \sqrt{3}$.
A $\sqrt{12} \times \sqrt{3} = \sqrt{12 \times 3}$
$= \sqrt{36}$
$= 6$

rationalisation of: The process of removing a surd from the **denominator** of a fraction. See also **surd**, **conjugate**, on the previous page.

Q1 Rationalise $\dfrac{5}{2\sqrt{3}}$.

A $\dfrac{5}{2\sqrt{3}} \times \dfrac{\sqrt{3}}{\sqrt{3}} = \dfrac{5\sqrt{3}}{2\sqrt{9}}$

$= \dfrac{5\sqrt{3}}{6}$

Q2 Rationalise $\dfrac{5}{2\sqrt{3} + \sqrt{2}}$.

A $\dfrac{5}{2\sqrt{3} + \sqrt{2}} \times \dfrac{2\sqrt{3} - \sqrt{2}}{2\sqrt{3} - \sqrt{2}} = \dfrac{5(2\sqrt{3} - \sqrt{2})}{(2\sqrt{3})^2 - (\sqrt{2})^2}$

$= \dfrac{5(2\sqrt{3} - \sqrt{2})}{12 - 2}$

$= \dfrac{2\sqrt{3} - \sqrt{2}}{2}$

simplification: This involves a reversal of multiplication to identify factors of a surd that have an exact square root.

Q Simplify: $\sqrt{32} + \sqrt{8}$
A $\sqrt{32} + \sqrt{8} = \sqrt{16 \times 2} + \sqrt{4 \times 2}$
$= \sqrt{16} \times \sqrt{2} + \sqrt{4} \times \sqrt{2}$
$= 4\sqrt{2} + 2\sqrt{2}$
$= 6\sqrt{2}$

subtraction: Only like terms can be subtracted.

Q Find $\sqrt{12} - \sqrt{3}$.
A $\sqrt{12} - \sqrt{3} = 2\sqrt{3} - \sqrt{3}$
$= \sqrt{3}$.

surface The outside layer of a solid shape. A surface can be flat or curved.

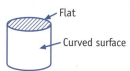

surface area of a solid The total area of the faces of a solid found by calculation of the area of each face or surface and then add these together. **Formulae** exist for many of the common solids, as below.

Cube

$SA = 6s^2$

Rectangular prism
$SA = 2(lw + lh + hw)$

Cylinder
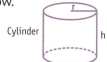
$SA = 2\pi r^2 + 2\pi rh$
$= 2\pi r(r + h)$

Pyramid

$SA = s^2 + 4 \times \frac{1}{2}sl$
$= s^2 + 2sl$

Sphere

$SA = 4\pi r^3$

Triangular pyramid
SA = sum of the area of 4 triangular faces

continued over

S Surface area of a solid

Q1 Find the surface area of a cube of side 6 cm.
A $SA = 6s^2$
$= 6 \times 6^2$
$= 216$ cm^2

Q2 Find the surface area.
A $SA = 2(lw + lh + wh)$
$= 2 \times (9 \times 4 + 9 \times 6 + 4 \times 6)$
$= 2 \times 114$
$= 228$ cm^2

Q3 Find the surface area.

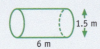

A $SA = 2\pi r(r + h)$
$= 2\pi \times 0.75(0.75 + 6)$
$= 31.81$ cm^2 (to 2 decimal places)

Q4 Find the surface area.

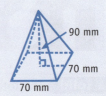

A First find the **slant height** of a face.
$l^2 = 35^2 + 90^2$
$\therefore l = \sqrt{9325}$
$= 96.6$ mm (to 1 decimal place)
$SA = s^2 + 2sl$
$= 70^2 + 2 \times 70 \times 96.6$
$= 18\,419$ mm^2

Note: If the base is a rectangle, two different slant heights will have to be found.

Q5 Find the surface area of a sphere of diameter 12.8 cm.
A Radius is half of the diameter.
$SA = 4\pi r^2$
$= 4 \times \pi \times (6.4)^2$
$= 514.7$ cm^2 (to 1 decimal place)

survey A general view or description. A form of data collection through the use of **interview** or **questionnaire** of a **representative sample** of the **population**. See these entries also.
Examples: *A transport survey or a survey of opinion.*

survey, land The accurate measurement of the dimensions and slopes of a piece of land. Carried out by a surveyor.

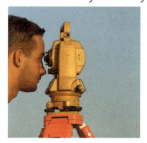 

surveyors' bearings Descriptions using the compass directions north, south, east and west and the subdivisions of these. See also **bearings** and **true bearings**.

symbols in mathematics The signs we use in mathematics. These are usually operations.
Examples: $+ \quad - \quad \times \quad \div \quad < \quad \leq \quad > \quad \geq \quad \neq \quad \equiv \quad \doteq \quad \propto \quad \pm$

symbols, grouping See **grouping symbols** and **brackets**.

symbolic Using marks or symbols that have a mathematical meaning.

symmetry A balanced arrangement. See also **reflection** and **axis of symmetry**.
line symmetry: Where one half of a figure is the mirror image of the other. See also **point symmetry** and **rotational symmetry**.

T — table

table An arrangement of data. See **frequency distribution (table)**, for example.

take away An instruction; meaning to **subtract**.

> **Q** Take away 7 from 15.
> **A** This means 15 − 7 = 8.

tally (marks) An instruction to use the data given to group them into a **table** using frequencies. Also means to find the total. See also **frequency**.
The tallies are grouped in fives by using ⋕

x	tally	f
10	⋕ II	7
20	⋕ ⋕ I	11
30	⋕ ⋕ III	13
40	⋕ IIII	9
50	III	3

tan The abbreviation and symbol for the **tangent ratio**, see next page.

tangent A straight line that touches but does not cross a curve at a point.

tangent to a circle Touches the circle at right angles to the **radius** of the circle at the point of contact.

tangent ratio

tangent ratio Used in **trigonometry** in a right-angled triangle. It is found by calculating the value $\frac{\text{opposite}}{\text{adjacent}}$. It is abbreviated **tan**.

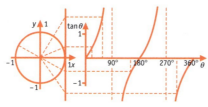

A graph can represent the values of the tangent of an angle for angle values from 0° to 360°.

tangram Shapes made with the seven tans (plane shapes cut from a square): An ancient Chinese puzzle.

tax bracket **Income** bands within which all earnings are taxed at a fixed rate.

Tax rates 2006–07

Taxable income	Tax on this income
$0–$6,000	nil
$6,001–$25,000	15c for each $1 over $6,000
$25,001–$75,000	$2,850 plus 30c for each $1 over $25,000
$75,001–$150,000	$17,850 plus 40c for each $1 over $75,000
over $150,000	$47,850 plus 45c for each $1 over $150,000

T tax deductions

tax deductions Legitimate expenses that reduce income because they are directly involved in increasing the capacity of an individual to earn an **income**.

tax rebate (refund) The amount repaid to the tax payer by the Australian Taxation Office (ATO) after the calculation of tax payable, when there is a surplus of taxation contributions.

taxable income The amount left after any deductions are made from gross income.

temperature The measurement of heat and cold through the use of a **thermometer**. Two scales are used: **Celsius** and **fahrenheit**. See these separate entries.

tens column or position The position in a **Hindu-Arabic numeral** that represents lots of 10.

Thousands	Hundreds	Tens	Units
4	5	8	3

The number in the tens position is 8.

> **Q** Give the value of the 7 in 376.
> **A** The number in expanded form is $3 \times 100 + 7 \times 10 + 6 \times 1$. Thus the 7 is 7 tens.

tenth An ordinal number.
1 2 3 4 5 6 7 8 9 10
1st 2nd 3rd 4th 5th 6th 7th 8th 9th 10th

One tenth $\left(\frac{1}{10}\right)$: One part in ten equal parts.

tenths column or position The position in a **Hindu-Arabic** decimal numeral that represents tenths ($\frac{1}{10}$).

Tens	Units	.	Tenths	Hundredths
5	4	.	9	3

The number in the tenths position is 9.

> **Q** Give the value of the 5 in 34.56.
> **A** The number in expanded form is
> $3 \times 10 + 4 \times 1 + 5 \times \frac{1}{10} + 6 \times \frac{1}{100}$.
> Thus the 5 is 5 tenths.

terminate To come to an end, to go no further.

terminating decimals A decimal that comes to an end (there is no remainder in the division). It has a definite number of places. $\frac{6}{10} = \frac{3}{5} = 0.6$; $1\frac{1}{4} = 1.25$; and $\frac{5}{8} = 0.625$ are examples.

term A part of an algebraic expression. See **expression, algebraic**. $3x^2 - 7x + 3$ is an expression of three terms. $3x^2$ is the leading term.

terms, buying on See **time payment**.

terms
like: Like terms are those with identical **pronumeral** parts.
unlike: Unlike terms are those that are different (ie not like terms).
$3x^2y$ and $7x^2y$ are **like** terms, while $3x^2y$ and $3xy^2$ are **unlike** terms.

tessellation A pattern created by the repetition of a shape or shapes with no gaps or overlapping. To fill all the space around a point where the boundaries meet.

T tetrahedron

tetrahedron A **triangular pyramid** where each face is a triangle. When all faces are equilateral triangles, the regular tetrahedron is one of the five **platonic solids**. See this entry also.

thermometer Measuring device to determine temperature. Measurements are in degrees in the **Celsius** and **fahrenheit** scales.

theodolite A surveyor's instrument for measuring angles in the horizontal or vertical plane.

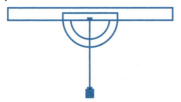 

theorem A statement (proposition) that can be proven using an **axiom** or other statement already proven to be true.

theoretical probability See **probability**.

three-dimensional (3D) The property of having **length**, **width** and **thickness**. Such objects are called **solids**. See these entries.

thickness One of the three dimensions. Often referred to as the **height**.

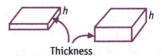

Thickness

third T

third An ordinal number, after second and before fourth. See **tenth** for diagram.

thousand Ten hundreds.
$1000 = 10^3$.
Note: K is often used informally as a short term for thousands in relation to money and other large numbers.
The cost was $35K

thousands column or position The position in a **Hindu-Arabic numeral** that represents lots of 1000.

Thousands	Hundreds	Tens	Units
4	5	8	3

The number in the thousands position is 4.

> **Q** Give the value of the 5 in 5376.
> **A** The number in expanded form is: $5 \times 1000 + 3 \times 100 + 7 \times 10 + 6 \times 1$.
> Thus the 5 is 5 thousands.

thousandths column or position The position in a **Hindu-Arabic** decimal numeral that represents thousandths $\left(\frac{1}{1000}\right)$.

Tens	Units	.	Tenths	Hundredths	Thousandths
4	5	.	8	3	7

The number in the thousandths position is 7.

> **Q** Give the value of the 7 in 34.567.
> **A** The number in expanded form is:
> $3 \times 10 + 4 \times 1 + 5 \times \frac{1}{10} + 6 \times \frac{1}{100} + 7 \times \frac{1}{1000}$.
> Thus the 7 is 7 thousandths.

three-digit bearing See **bearing**.

T time

time The measurement of the rotation of the Earth. Measured by clocks (analogue and digital). Units include the **second** (s), **minute** (min), **hour** (h), **day**, **week**, **month** and **year**. See these units.

60 s = 1 min   60 min = 1 h   24 h = 1 day
7 days = 1 week   14 days = 1 fortnight
4 weeks (approx) = 1 month   12 months = 1 year   365 days = 1 year
366 days = 1 leap year
Connected with distance and speed by the relationship: Time = $\dfrac{\text{Distance}}{\text{Speed}}$.

24-hour time: See **twenty-four-hour time**.
12-hour time: See **twelve-hour time**.
addition of: A variation of the addition algorithm is used.

> **Q** Add 2 h 23 min 42 s to 5 h 37 min 43 s.
> **A** The carrying numbers are 60 s = 1 min and
>   60 min = 1 h
>
> | | h | min | s |
> |---|---|---|---|
> | | 1 | 1 | |
> | | 2 | 23 | 42 |
> | + | 5 | 37 | 43 |
> | | 8 | 1 | 25 |
>
> The answer is 8 h 1 min 25 s.

subtraction of: A variation of the subtraction algorithm is used.

> **Q** Subtract 2 h 34 min 17 s from 5 h 22 min 13 s.
> **A** The carrying numbers are 60 s = 1 min and
>   60 min = 1 h
>
> | | h | min | s |
> |---|---|---|---|
> | | | 81 | |
> | | 4̶ | 2̶1̶ | 7̶3̶ |
> | | 5 | 22 | 13 |
> | − | 2 | 34 | 17 |
> | | 2 | 47 | 56 |
>
> The answer is 2 h 47 min 56 s.

time-and-a-half

calculator use: Enter hours, minutes and seconds with the ° ' " button (*Casio*) or the DMS button (*Sharp*).

Q Add 2 h 23 min 42 s to 5 h 37 min 43 s.
A Enter 2 ° ' " 23 ° ' " 42 ° ' " + 5 ° ' " 37 ° ' " 43 ° ' " = to give 8°1"25'

time-and-a-half A rate of pay for overtime. Calculated at one and a half times the standard rate. See also **hourly rate of pay**, **double time** and **penalty rates**.

time interval The time that passes between two events. See also **time**.

time line Representation of events that occurred over a period of time on an evenly divided line.

1970 1980 1990 2000 2010

time payment The purchasing of goods by entering into a contract to pay the value of the goods plus interest over a period of time. More correctly called 'leasing' under government legislation.

time series data A collection of data where one of the variables is time. An example is the increase in height of a hang glider in a rising thermal.

T time zones

time zones Regions of the Earth that are considered to have the same time. They are usually based on a capital city. In Australia there are three time zones: EST (Eastern Standard Time in Qld, NSW, ACT, Vic, Tas); CST (Central Standard Time in SA, NT); and WST (Western Standard Time in WA). See also **daylight saving time**.

times (×) A term for **multiplication**

> **Q** Find 2 times 3.
> **A** This means 2 × 3 and the result is 6.

timetable A presentation of events over a period of time. Usually presented as a rectangular arrangement. Examples include class timetables, train and bus timetables and TV program guides.

tonne (t) A unit of **mass** in the **SI system**, equal to one thousand kilograms.

1000 kg = 1 t

top view The view of a **solid** from above. One of the **orthogonal** views. See this entry also.

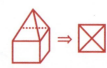

topological map A map of a portion of the Earth's surface that shows the features of the landscape such as rivers, lakes and oceans; hills and mountains using contour lines; roads and towns using symbols.

topology A branch of mathematics concerned with relationships rather than measurements: Inside and outside, surfaces, shapes and connections. See also **network**.

The cup and the donut have one hole in their surfaces and so are topologically the same.

torus A three-dimensional (3D) shape, such as a donut or a tube. Important in **topology**, above.

total The result of **addition**.

> **Q** Find the total of 7 and 8
> **A** This means $7 + 8 = 15$. Thus the total is 15.

Tower of Hanoi A puzzle consisting of three posts fixed to a base, together with a set of discs of increasing diameters. The object of the game is to move the discs one at a time from their position in decreasing size to another post, again in decreasing size. At no time can a disc be placed over another that is smaller in diameter.

transcendental numbers

transcendental numbers An irrational number that is not a **surd**. See **irrational numbers** also. An example is π.

transformation A change or movement.
algebra: The changes associated with the basic parabola $y = x^2$. The transformations are: narrow – widen (**dilation**); left – right (**translation**) and up – down (translation).

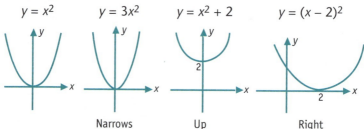

$y = x^2$ $y = 3x^2$ $y = x^2 + 2$ $y = (x - 2)^2$
             Narrows   Up   Right

geometry: General name for movements in a plane, where there is **one-to-one correspondence** between the object and the image. Examples include **dilation** (enlargement), **reflection**, **rotation** and **translation**, below. See these entries.

translation The movement of a **plane shape** in a straight line. Size and orientation are unchanged.

transposition The process of rearranging a **formula** to make a particular **pronumeral** (variable) the subject of the formula. See also subject, change of. $E = \frac{1}{2}mv^2$ can be transposed to give $v = \sqrt{\frac{2E}{m}}$.

transversal The line that crosses at least two other lines. Especially used with an **oblique** cut of **parallel lines**. See this entry.

trapezium A **quadrilateral** with a pair of parallel sides.

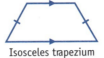
Isosceles trapezium

trapezium, area of See **area of, trapezium**.

trapezoid Confusion exists about the use of this word. Modern Australian usage indicates it is an alternative to trapezium. See especially its use as **trapezoidal**, below, to describe solids with trapeziums as surfaces.

trapezoidal An object having a trapezium as a surface. **prism:** A prism with a cross-section of a **trapezium**, see above.

travel graphs Line graphs that show time as the **independent variable** and distance as the **dependent variable**. They are an example of a **rate**. See this entry also.

traversable A network is traversable if it can be traced without lifting the pen or going over the same part of the curve more than once. See also **networks**.

Traversable

Not traversable

treble To multiply by 3.
In 10 years the value of the property has trebled. It was $100 000 and is now $300 000.

tree diagram A branching graph without loops used to represent outcomes in **probability**. Also used to show prime factorisation. See also **prime factors**.

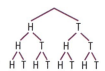

$16 = 2 \times 2 \times 2 \times 2 = 2^4$

triads, pythagorean See **pythagorean triads**.

trial In **statistics**, a single event or **observation**.

trial and error A method of solving **equations** by making an estimate of the result, then substituting that value to enable a second, more refined, estimate and so on. Also called **guess, check and refine**.

triangle A plane three-sided figure. See separate entries for **acute-angled triangle**, **equilateral triangle**, **isosceles triangle**, **obtuse-angled triangle**, **right-angled triangle** and **scalene triangle**.
The angle sum of a triangle is 180°. See separate entries for **area, of triangle**, **exterior angle** and **similar triangle tests** and **congruent triangles**.

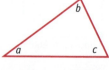

$a + b + c = 180°$

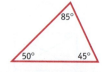

$50° + 45° + 85° = 180°$

triangular numbers Numbers that can be represented by dots arranged in triangles. See also **square numbers**.

1, 3, 6, 10, 15 are the first 5 triangular numbers.

triangular numbers, relationship with square numbers The second square number is the sum of the first two triangular numbers, the third square numbers is the sum of the second and third triangular numbers, and so on.

$1 + 3 = 4 = 2^2$
$3 + 6 = 9 = 3^2$
$6 + 10 = 16 = 4^2$

triangular prism A **prism** with a triangular base.

triangular pyramid A **pyramid** with a triangular base. See also **tetrahedron**.

triangulation A method of fixing a point in a plane by taking bearings of that point from two known points.

trigonometric identities

trigonometric identities Mathematical statements involving **sin θ**, **cos θ** and **tan θ** that are true for all values of θ. Examples include:
$\tan\theta = \frac{\sin\theta}{\cos\theta}$, $\cos\theta \neq 0$; $\sin 2\theta = 2\sin\theta\cos\theta$; $\sin^2\theta + \cos^2\theta = 1$
$\cos 2\theta = \cos^2\theta - \sin^2\theta = 2\cos^2\theta - 1 = 1 - 2\sin^2\theta$

trigonometric ratios See separate entries for **cosine ratio**, **sine ratio** and **tangent ratio**.

trigonometry A branch of **geometry** that is used to find sides and angles in triangles both right-angled and non right-angled. Trigonometry has many applications in navigation, surveying, engineering, astronomy and architecture. See also **cosine ratio**, **cosine rule**, **sine ratio**, **sine rule** and **tangent ratio**.
Note: There are many developments of trigonometry as functions that are studied in senior school and in higher education.

trillion In modern Australian usage, a million million. Originally a million million million in imperial usage.
$1\,000\,000\,000\,000 = 10^{12}$

trinomial expression An expression with three terms. See also **quadratic trinomials**.
$7x^2 + 6x - 5$ is a quadratic trinomial.
$7x + 3y + z$ is a trinomial expression.

trisect In geometry; to divide into three equal parts.

true bearing The angle measured clockwise from North to the direction being considered. Always given in the form 135°T (as 3 digits). See also **surveyors' bearings**.

Truncation — T

truncation Cutting off. For example, a *trapezium* is a truncated triangle. See also *frustum*.

turn See *rotation*.

turning point form A way to express the *quadratic equation* as $y = a(x - h)^2 + k$. The turning point is (h, k).

twelve-hour time Recording time from the analog clock that uses only the digits 1 to 12. Afternoon is given as pm and morning as am. See also *twenty-four hour time*, *analog time* and *digital time*.

> **Q** Give 1730 hours in 12-hour time.
> **A** 1730 = 1200 + 530. Thus 1730 hours = 5:30 pm.

Twenty-four hour time The method of recording time that divides a calendar day into 24 time periods, each of one hour. Used to avoid confusion over am and pm. Also known as military time, where it was first introduced. Now used in most parts of Europe and in all airline and much other travel scheduling. See also *digital time*.

> **Q** Give 3:30 pm in 24-hour time.
> **A** 3:30 pm is
> 1200 + 0330 = 1530 hours in 24-hour time.

Twice To multiply by two.
One candle is twice as tall as the other candle.

two-dimensional (2D) Figures that have length and width but no thickness.

two-intercept method The method of drawing a straight line by plotting the **intercepts** on each **axis**. The intercepts found by the substitution of $x = 0$ for the **y-intercept** and $y = 0$ for the **x-intercept**.

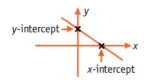

two mean regression line A **regression line** designed to fit bivariate data. The data is divided into two halves and the mean of the x and y values are calculated separately for both halves and then plotted. The join of these two points is the required line. See also **data, bivariate**.

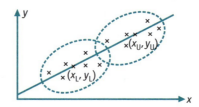

u An abbreviation for units. Used when a specific unit of measurement is not given.

> **Q** Find the perimeter of the figure.
> **A** The perimeter is given by $P = 2(l + b) = 2(3 + 4) = 14$ u.

uncommon units of measure Prefixes are used for very large and very small measurements. The prefixes most commonly used are:

nano (n): $10^{-9} = \dfrac{1}{1\,000\,000\,000}$

micro (µ): $10^{-6} = \dfrac{1}{1\,000\,000}$

mega (M): $10^6 = 1\,000\,000$

giga (G): $10^9 = 1\,000\,000\,000$.

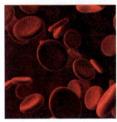

Red blood cells are 7.82 microns in diameter and 2.58 microns thick.
1 micron = 10^{-6} metre.

undefined term A **term** or expression taken as accepted without **definition**.

unequal (≠) Not equal to, not the same value. $3 \times 4 \neq 11$

unfair game A game where the probability of success and the probability of failure favour the person running the game. Most gambling games are in this category to ensure the operator of the game makes a **profit**.

ungrouped data Data which is not grouped into classes. See also **data, grouped**.

uniform 1 Unchanged. The circumstances remain the same over time.
2 An alternative to the use of **regular**. See this entry also.

uniform cross-section When the **cross sections** of a **solid** taken parallel to the base are always the same size and shape. Applies to and identifies **prisms**.

uniform rate

uniform rate A rate that is unchanged over time. See **average rate** and **rate**.
Betty was paid a uniform rate of $18 per hour for her holiday job.

union (set) (∪) The region formed in a **Venn diagram** when two sets are combined.

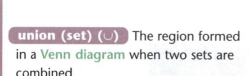

A ∪ B is the shaded region

unique One of a kind, unlike any other. Often refers to a result in an **equation**. See this entry also.
$x = 3$ is the unique result to $4x + 2 = 14$, while $x^2 = 16$ has two answers $+4$ and -4, neither of which is the unique answer for the equation.

unit 1 A basic construct for counting or measurement. For example the **metre** is the basic unit of measurement of length. See also **SI system** of measurement.
2 Another name for 1. See also **place value**.

unit circle A circle of **radius** one unit. Used in **trigonometry** for angles of any magnitude.

unit fraction A fraction that has a **numerator** of the number one.
Examples: $\frac{1}{2}, \frac{1}{3}$ and $\frac{1}{4}$.

unit of measurement

unit of measurement All quantities are measured with the appropriate units. See separate entries for **length**, **area** (square), **volume** (cubic), **capacity**, **mass**, **time**, **temperature**, and **astronomical unit**. See also **measurement**.

unit of measurement, standard See **metric system**.

unit rate The assessment of the value of a single unit of a material in order to make comparisons easier between quantities. See also **unitary method**.

unit square A square with sides equal to one unit of length. See also **units for area and volume**, next page.

unitary method A method used to solve problems that involve quantities by finding the value of one quantity first.

Q1 If 7 books cost $42, find the cost of 9 books.
A One book costs 42 ÷ 7 = 6. Thus 9 books cost $6 × 9 = $54.

Q2 If 5 people take 4 days to complete a job, how long will it take 7 people working at the same rate?
A One person takes 5 × 4 = 20 days. Thus 7 will take 20 ÷ 7 = $2\frac{6}{7}$ days.

Note: The first method, which involves cost, uses division to find the unit amount while the second, which involves time, uses multiplication to find the unit amount of time.

U units column or position

units column or position The position in a **Hindu-Arabic numeral** that represents ones or units.

Thousands	Hundreds	Tens	Units
4	5	8	3

The number in the units position is 3.

> **Q** Give the value of the 6 in 376.
> **A** The number in expanded form is $3 \times 100 + 7 \times 10 + 6 \times 1$. Thus the 6 is 6 ones.

units for area and volume When there are no length units given, **area** should be expressed as square units (u^2) and **volume** as cubic units (u^3). See **u** also.

unity An alternative name for the number 1.

univariate data See **data, univariate**.

universal set (ξ) The set of all possible elements or objects considered in a particular situation. In a **Venn diagram** this is shown as a rectangle enclosing the remainder of the diagram.
When selecting letters of the alphabet, the universal set would be the total alphabet.

unknown value In **algebraic expressions**, **equations** and **inequations**, the unknown value is represented by a symbol, variable or pronumeral.

$3 \times \square = 12$	$2x - 6 \leq 8$	$3x - 4b$
Unknown	Unknown (variable)	Unknowns (pronumerals)

unlike terms Terms that are different. See also **like terms**.

$5a - 3b$	$4x + x$
Unlike terms	Like terms

UTC Universal Time Coordinate. Alternative name for Greenwich Mean Time (GMT). See **longitude**.

V Symbol for **volume**. See this entry.

value 1 When an **equation** is solved the result is the value of the **pronumeral**. If $5x - 2 = 18$, then the value of the equation is 4 as $5 \times 4 - 2 = 18$.
2 An amount. The value of an **expression**.

> **Q** Find the value of $5x - 2$ when $x = 4$.
> **A** Substitute $x = 4$: $5 \times 4 - 2 = 18$. Thus the value is 18.

vanishing point Used in **perspective drawing**. See this entry.

variable A letter or symbol that stands for a number in an **expression**, **equation** or **inequation**. An arbitrary element of a set. It can vary. See **arbitrary (free) variable**. See also **pronumeral**.
dependent: The variable that is obtained after substitution of the independent variable into an equation. Plotted on the **vertical axis** of the number plane.
independent: The variable that can be freely chosen from an appropriate set of values.
In $y = 7x + 3$, x is the independent variable and y is the dependent variable.

variable expenses Payments for clothing, food and entertainment. Used in the calculation of a budget. See also **budget** and **fixed expenses**.

variation The movement of one variable relative to another. This can be either direct (moving in the same direction) or inverse (moving in the opposite direction). See entries for **direct variation (or proportion)** and **inverse variation (or proportion)**.

Venn Diagram Named after John Venn, 1834-1923, English logician. A logic diagram that uses two or more circles inside a rectangle to represent a set and its subsets. The circles may or may not overlap. See also **universal set**, **union**, **intersection** and **chance, Venn diagrams**.

V vertex

vertex 1 The turning point of a curve such as a **parabola**.

2 The point where two sides meet in a plane figure.

3 A point in space where several edges meet but do not extend beyond.

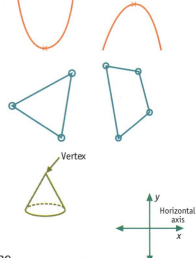

vertical axis In a graph or a number plane, the top-bottom axis. See also **horizontal axis**.

vertical line A line at right angles to the horizontal. The general form of the equation is: $x = k$, where k is a constant.

vertical line test for a function: If a vertical line cuts the graph of a **relation** once only for all values in its **domain**, then the relation is a **function**.

Function

Not a function

vertically opposite angles Angles formed by the **intersection** of two straight lines. The orientation is unimportant. These angles are equal.

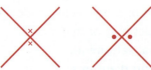

vertices Plural of **vertex**. See this entry, previous page.

vinculum The line between the **numerator** and **denominator** in a **fraction**. See these entries also.

$$\frac{4}{7} \leftarrow \text{Vinculum}$$

volume The measure of the amount of material in a **solid**. There are standard formulae to calculate volumes of many solids, as follows. See also **capacity**.

of a cone: $V = \frac{1}{3}\pi r^2 h$

Q Find the volume of the cone.
A $V = \frac{1}{3}\pi r^2 h$
$= \frac{1}{3}\pi \times 5^2 \times 8$
$= 209.4$ cm³ (to 1 decimal place)

of a cylinder: $V = \pi r^2 h$

Q Find the volume of the cylinder.
A $V = \pi r^2 h$
$= \pi \times 6^2 \times 9$
$= 1017.9$ cm³ (to 1 decimal place)

of a prism: V = area base times height, or $V = l \times w \times h$.
$= lwh$

Q Find the volume of the prism.
A $V = lwh$
$= 9 \times 8 \times 7$
$= 504$ cm³

V volume

of a pyramid: V = one third of the area of the base times the height, or
$V = \frac{1}{3} l \times w \times h$
$= \frac{1}{3} lwh$

Q Find the volume of the pyramid.

A $V = \frac{1}{3} lwh$
$= \frac{1}{3} \times 7 \times 9 \times 11$
$= 231$ cm³

of a sphere: V = four thirds of π times the **radius** cubed, or $V = \frac{4}{3}\pi r^3$

Q Find the volume of a sphere of radius 11.5 m.

A $V = \frac{4}{3}\pi r^3$
$= \frac{4}{3}\pi \times (11.5)^3$
$= 6370.6$ m³ (to 1 decimal place)

of compound solids: Add the separate parts to get the total volume.

Q Find the volume of the solid.

A The solid consists of a prism and a pyramid
$V = \frac{1}{3} lwh + lwh$
Thus $= \frac{1}{3} \times 7 \times 4 \times 8 + 7 \times 4 \times 5$
$= 214\frac{2}{3}$ cm³

vulgar fraction See **fraction**.

wage Payment for work done in employment. Calculated on an hourly rate of pay. See also **salary**, **royalties** and **overtime**.

> Q Find the weekly wage for 38 hours regular work and 3 hours at time-and-a-half when the hourly rate is $15.20.
> A $38 \times 15.20 + 3 \times 1.5 \times 15.20 = 646$. Thus the wage is $646.

week A period of 7 days.

weight The force that an object exerts on the Earth. It is closely related to **mass**. There is a variation due to height above sea level. Astronaughts in space have no weight yet their mass is unchanged.

weighted mean The **mean** calculated by the use of weights or frequencies.

> Q Find the mean mass of 30 tins of beans if 15 contain 200 g, 8 contain 225 g and the rest contain 450 g.
> A Weighted mean = $\dfrac{15 \times 200 + 8 \times 225 + 7 \times 450}{30}$
> = 265 g.

whole The sum of the parts. $\dfrac{10}{10} = 1$

Gives

whole numbers Zero and the counting numbers. 0, 1, 2, 3, 4, 5, . . .

width The distance from side to side. Also called breadth.

write An instruction which means to give the answer on paper, often in a sentence rather than just as a number or letter.
For example, *write a rule* means give an **equation** in **algebra**.

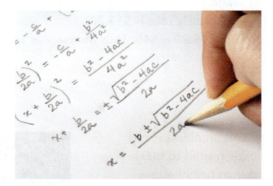

x x and other letters are used as **variables** in **algebra**. x is by far the most common letter used for an unknown.
$P(x) = x^4 - 7x^2 + 3x - 5$ is a polynomial with x as the variable.

x-axis The **horizontal axis** in the number plane. See also **coordinates**.

x coordinate The first value in a number pair, which is the distance from the **origin** on the *x*-axis. See also **coordinates**.

x-intercept The value cut off on the *x*-axis by a graph. See also **y-intercept**. The *x*-intercept is found from an **equation** by substituting $y = 0$.

The *x*-intercept is 2.

The *x*-intercepts are 0 and 4.

continued over

X x-intercept

Q1 Find the *x-intercept* for $3x + 5y = 15$.

A When $y = 0$, $3x + 5y = 15$ becomes $3x + 5 \times 0 = 15$.
This gives $x = 5$.

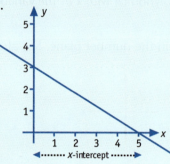

Q2 Find the *x-intercepts* of $y = x^2 + 5x - 6$.

A $y = x^2 + 5x - 6$ becomes $x^2 + 5x - 6 = 0 = (x + 6)(x - 1)$
Thus $x + 6 = 0$ or $x - 1 = 0$ and the intercepts are $x = -6$ and $x = 1$.

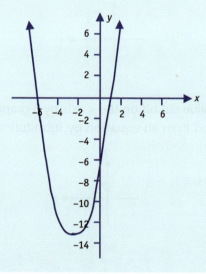

y y and other letters are used as **variables** in **algebra**. After *x* it is the most common letter used for an unknown.
$y = 7x^2 + 3x - 5$ is a **quadratic** with *x* as the **independent variable** and *y* as the **dependent variable**.

y-axis The **vertical axis** in the **number plane**. See also **coordinates**.

yard **Imperial unit** of length. Approximately 91 cm.

y-coordinate The second value in a **number pair**, which is the distance from the **origin** on the *y*-axis.

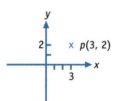

Year The period of time it takes for the Earth to pass around the Sun. The **leap year** is the allowance for the fact that the actual time taken is 365 days, 5 hours and 48.75 minutes. See this entry also.

Y *y-intercept*

y-intercept The value cut off on the *y-axis* by a graph. See also *x-intercept*.

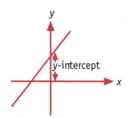
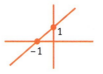

Q1 Find the *y-intercept* for $3x + 5y = 15$.

A When $x = 0$, $3x + 5y = 15$
becomes $3 \times 0 + 5y = 15$.
This gives $y = 3$.

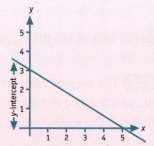

Q2 Find the *y-intercept* for the equation $y = x^2 - 5x + 6$.

A When $x = 0$, $y = 0^2 - 5 \times 0 + 6 = 6$
Thus the *y-intercept* is 6.

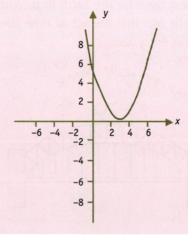

z-angles Another name for **alternate angles**. See this entry.

Zeno's paradoxes Zeno was a Greek who lived in the 5th century BC. He proposed a number of contradictory problems called paradoxes that illustrate various mathematical concepts in time, space, motion, limits and **infinity**. For an example see **Achilles and the Tortoise**.

Zero The numeral 0. Used as a place holder in numerals. Occupies the space between the positive and negative numbers. Also called nought, nothing, nil and none.
. . . , –4, –3, –2, –1, 0, +1, +2, +3, +4, . . .
3405 indicates there are 3 thousands, 4 hundreds, **no** tens and 5 ones.
Note: The invention of zero allowed the development of place value and thus all modern calculations through the use of **algorithms**.

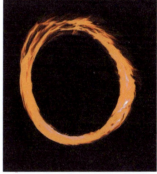

zero index Any expression raised to the zero index is equal to 1. See **index operations**.
$a^0 = 1$, $a \neq 0$.
$(3x^2y^{-2})^0 = 1$, as does $123456789^0 = 1$.

zero, multiply by When any value is multiplied by zero the value is zero. Thus there are no divisors of zero.
$6 \times 0 = 0 \times 6 = 0$ $a \times 0 = 0$